The Incredible
HOCKEY QUIZ
Challenge

Ron Wight

Foreword by Brian McFarlane

National Library of Canada Cataloguing in Publication

Wight, Ron
        The incredible hockey quiz challenge / Ron Wight.

ISBN 1-894933-51-6

        1. Hockey--Miscellanea. 2. National Hockey League--Miscellanea.
I. Title.

GV847.W4925 2003   796.962'64   C2003-906642-8

Volumes Publishing Limited
907 Frederick Street, Unit 5
Kitchener, Ontario
Canada N2B 2B9

www.volpub.com

Printed in Canada

*This book is dedicated
to everyone who loves hockey.
May the game give you
the same enjoyment it has given me.*

The Incredible Hockey Quiz Challenge

TABLE OF CONTENTS

FOREWORD

In more than half a century as a hockey broadcaster and author, I have met few hockey fans who don't enjoy playing hockey trivia. A couple of my favourite trivia questions come to mind. What were Bobby Hull's jersey numbers before he adopted number 9? The answer: 7 and 16.

Who holds the NHL record for scoring the fastest goal by a rookie. The same player holds the record for the fastest three assists in a game. The answer; Gus Bodnar, now 80, and his records (15 seconds as a Leaf and 21 seconds as a Black Hawk) have lasted for more than 50 years.

An amazing amount of hockey trivia and information is stored in the recesses of the brain of author Ron Wight. Even he can't explain how it got there and why it remains there. But it's always on call. It must be fun to have hundreds of little hockey players running around in your cranium all day, and being able be to identify them by number and team and even personality quirks, citing drafts and trades that got them where they are and recalling amazing feats and records that made them famous. Or, conversely, the lack of ability that made them rather obscure.

Ron Wight knows his hockey. And hockey trivia is his game. It's always a delight when he shares his knowledge of our favourite winter sport with his thousands of readers.

Brian McFarlane
Hockey Hall of Fame, 1995

ACKNOWLEDGEMENTS

A book can never be written without the help of many who contribute to its development. There are several people involved with this project that deserve recognition.

I would like to thank Brian McFarlane for writing the foreword. Brian has been an inspiration to me since I was a child. I greatly appreciate his kind words.

The pictures in the book have been used with the permission of Bruce Bennett Studios. The staff was very professional and eager to assist me.

I also appreciate the hard work and cooperation of Dean Froome and the staff at Volumes Publishing. They have made a significant contribution to the production of this book.

Most importantly, I would like to thank my family. I could never have completed this project without the tremendous efforts of my daughters. Carly put countless hours into word processing the manuscript, and Jodie served as proof reader. A very special thank you to Cindy, my teammate for life, for all her love and support.

Ron Wight
August 2003

INTRODUCTION

I recently looked back over hockey scrapbooks I made as a child. With intricate detail, I catalogued every player and team. What was it about the game that captivated me so much? Hockey trivia has been a part of my life for almost as long as I can remember. I still recall analyzing every detail of my first hockey book, one written by Brian McFarlane. He opened up a whole new world to me, one that I'm still exploring. These memories bring back the days of my childhood, but hockey still fills my life with enjoyment. Whether coaching or watching the game, I am removed from everyday cares to a place where, for the moment, the quest for the puck is all that matters.

This is my third book of hockey trivia. There are endless details to the game: past players and teams, present day trends and future predictions. Hockey has changed and will continue to do so. I try to appreciate every minute of my life, no matter what I am doing. Somehow, those spent in the world of hockey are special. I hope you have fun with The Incredible Hockey Quiz Challenge. It has been quite a journey.

Ron Wight
www.hockeyovertime.com

The World of Hockey

Hockey truly has become a global game. The last decade saw several countries step into the forefront of world competition. The United States won the first-ever World Cup of Hockey in 1996 and also captured the inaugural gold medal in women's Olympic hockey in 1998. The Czech Republic claimed the men's Olympic gold medal in 1998 and had dominant performances in several World Championships and World Junior tournaments at the turn of the century. Recently, Russia has twice taken the gold in the World Junior Championship. Canada regained considerable hockey pride with a double gold medal performance at the 2002 Olympics and again with a gold in the men's 2003 World Championship. Hockey fans have plenty to look forward to in upcoming international events, especially the 2004 World Cup of Hockey.

FIRST PERIOD - OH CANADA

1. When was the last time the United States defeated Canada in men's Olympic hockey?

The last time the United States defeated Canada in Olympic men's hockey was February 25, 1960 when the Americans outscored the Canadians 2-1. The States won their first-ever gold medal in hockey at these Olympics, with Canada taking the silver and the Soviet Union the bronze. Since that 1960 match, Canada has a record of five wins and one tie in the six games played between the two countries in men's Olympic hockey.

2. How many times was Wayne Gretzky the leading scorer in a Canada Cup tournament?

Wayne Gretzky was the leading scorer in all four Canada Cups in which he participated.

Wayne Gretzky's Canada Cup Scoring Totals

Year	GP	G	A	PTS
1981	7	5	7	12
1984	8	5	7	12
1987	9	3	18	21
1991	7	4	8	12

3. Name the goaltender with an incredible record of 17-1-2 in the twenty games he played for Canada in international competitions during the early 1990s.

Bill Ranford had six wins and two ties with Team Canada in the 1991 Canada Cup. Ranford was named MVP of the tournament for his outstanding goaltending. He returned to international competition with Canada in 1993, recording five wins and a single loss at the World Championship. The following year he was the winner in six games as he led Canada to their first gold medal at a men's World Championship since 1961.

4. How many sweater numbers were shared by players on both the men's and women's 2002 Canadian Olympic hockey teams?

There were five sweater numbers shared by the two Canadian Olympic hockey teams.

Number	Men's Team	Women's Team
4	Rob Blake	Becky Kellar
11	Owen Nolan	Cheryl Pounder
12	Jarome Iginla	Lori Dupuis
25	Joe Nieuwendyk	Tammy Lee Shewchuk
91	Joe Sakic	Geraldine Heaney

5. Name the only Canadian-born player to have been awarded the Maurice "Rocket" Richard Trophy.

Jarome Iginla of the Calgary Flames received the Richard Trophy as the NHL's leading goal scorer for the 2001-02 season.

6. Name the player who took part in his fifth consecutive World Championship for Canada in 2003.

Ryan Smyth has competed for Canada in every men's World Hockey Championship between 1999 and 2003.

7. Name the two Canadian players who scored six seconds apart in the 2002 Olympics.

Hayley Wickenheiser and Jayna Hefford scored six seconds apart for the Canadian women's team in their semi-final game against Finland. This is a record in women's Olympic hockey. The goals came early in the third period to allow Canada to take a 4-3 lead en route to a 7-3 victory.

8. Who were the oldest and youngest players on the men's Canadian hockey team at the 2002 Winter Olympics?

Al MacInnis was thirty-eight years old when he played for Canada in the 2002 Winter Olympics. Simon Gagne, who was just shy of his twenty-second birthday, was the youngest.

9. Name the only WHA player to see ice time as a member of Team Canada at the 1976 Canada Cup.

Bobby Hull of the Winnipeg Jets was the only non-NHL player to see any game action with Canada in this tournament. Hull was Canada's leading goal scorer with five, which included three game winners. He recorded eight points in seven games in the 1976 Canada Cup.

10. Name the three players who were members of Team Canada at the men's World Championship in both 1997 and 2003.

Anson Carter, Sean Burke and Cory Cross skated on the gold medal-winning team at both the 1997 and 2003 World Championship.

11. Name the two members of the 1984 Canadian Olympic team who were still playing as regulars in the 2002-03 NHL season.

Kirk Muller and James Patrick were both members of Team Canada, which finished fourth at the 1984 Winter Olympics in Sarajevo, Yugoslavia. In 2002-03, Patrick played defense in sixty-nine games for the Buffalo Sabres, while forward Kirk Muller played in fifty-five regular season games and all twelve playoff games for the Dallas Stars.

12. Name the last NHL season in which all members of the First All-Star Team were Canadian-born.

The 1990-91 season was the last time that all six members of the NHL First All-Star Team were Canadian-born.

1990-91 NHL First All-Star Team

Player	Team	Position	Birthplace
Ed Belfour	Chicago	goal	Carman, Manitoba
Ray Bourque	Boston	defense	Montreal, Quebec
Al MacInnis	Calgary	defense	Inverness, Nova Scotia
Wayne Gretzky	Los Angeles	center	Brantford, Ontario
Brett Hull	St. Louis	right wing	Belleville, Ontario
Luc Robitaille	Los Angeles	left wing	Montreal, Quebec

13. Name the four Hart Trophy winners who were members of the Canadian Olympic team in 2002.

Eric Lindros, Mario Lemieux, Chris Pronger and Joe Sakic. Lemieux won the award on three occasions: 1988, 1993 and 1996. Lindros received the Hart as a member of the Flyers in 1995. Chris Pronger was presented with the trophy in 2000 and Joe Sakic had the honor in 2001.

14. Name the four individuals with extensive NHL careers who were also elected as federal members of the Canadian Parliament.

Lionel Conacher, Wilfred "Bucko" McDonald, Howie Meeker and Leonard "Red" Kelly all had lengthy careers in the National Hockey League and also served as federal members in the Canadian Parliament. Ex-NHLer Frank Mahovlich is presently a member of the Senate in Ottawa.

15. Name the six members of the Edmonton Oilers who skated with Team Canada at the 2003 World Championship.

Eric Brewer, Cory Cross, Mike Comrie, Shawn Horcoff, Steve Staios and Ryan Smyth were all members of the gold medal-winning Team Canada at the 2003 World Championship.

16. When was the last time that Canadian-born players won the Calder Trophy as the top NHL rookie in three consecutive seasons?

The last time this occurred was between 1977-78 and 1979-80.

Season	Player	Team	Birthplace
1977-78	Mike Bossy	New York Islanders	Montreal, Quebec
1978-79	Bobby Smith	Minnesota North Stars	North Sydney, Nova Scotia
1979-80	Ray Bourque	Boston Bruins	Montreal, Quebec

17. When did the opposition finally score on the Canadian women's Olympic hockey team in the 2002 competition?

Finland was the first team to score on the Canadian women's team. This did not occur until 19:35 of the first period of the semi-final game, which was the fourth game of the Olympic tournament for Team Canada. Canada had shutout Kazakhstan by a score of 7-0 to open the tournament, followed by a 7-0 victory over Russia and an 11-0 win over Sweden. During the semi-final game, Finland scored two more goals in the second period, but Canada came from behind to defeat them 7-3. This victory set up Canada's gold medal match with Team USA.

18. Name the only player to have skated with Team Canada in a Canada Cup tournament before playing in an NHL game.

Eric Lindros was a member of Team Canada '91 even though he had not seen action in an NHL game. Lindros had been the first overall pick by the Quebec Nordiques in the NHL Entry Draft earlier that year. He did not look out of place as he recorded three goals and two assists for five points in his eight games at the tournament. Lindros did not sign with Quebec, but went on to represent Canada at the Olympics, as well as the World Junior Championship, in the 1991-92 season.

19. Name the four Canadian players to be named the MVP of a Canada Cup tournament.

MVP	Canada Cup
Bobby Orr	1976
John Tonelli	1984
Wayne Gretzky	1987
Bill Ranford	1991

20. Name the two players who scored overtime winners for Team Canada at the 2003 World Championship in Finland.

The Canadians won their quarter-final match 3-2 over Germany when Eric Brewer scored thirty-seven seconds into extra time. Canada's other overtime winner came in the gold medal game when Anson Carter scored at 13:49 to give Canada a 3-2 victory over Sweden.

SECOND PERIOD - THE STARS AND STRIPES

1. How many times has the United States won a medal in men's Olympic hockey?

The United States has won a total of nine medals in the men's Olympic hockey events held between 1924 and 2002. The most recent was a silver medal won at the 2002 Winter Olympics in Salt Lake City. The Americans also won a silver medal in hockey at the 1920 Olympics held in Antwerp, Belgium, where men's hockey was played as a demonstration sport.

2. Name the three members of the 1998 American Olympic team who were former Calder Trophy winners.

Player	Team	Calder Trophy Year
Gary Suter	Calgary Flames	1985-86
Brian Leetch	New York Rangers	1988-89
Bryan Berard	New York Islanders	1996-97

3. Name the member of the gold medal-winning hockey team at the 1960 Olympics who went on to play over 600 games in the National Hockey League.

Tommy Williams of Duluth, Minnesota, recorded four goals and six assists in seven games with the American team at the 1960 Winter Olympics. Williams later saw action in thirteen NHL seasons with the Boston Bruins, the Minnesota North Stars, the California Golden Seals and the Washington Capitals. He also spent two seasons with the New England Whalers of the WHA. Williams recorded 161 goals and 430 points in 663 regular season NHL games over his career. He was honored in 1981 as a member of the United States Hockey Hall of Fame in Eveleth, Minnesota.

4. When was the first time that four American NHL franchises qualified for the Stanley Cup playoffs?

In 1929, the Boston Bruins, the Detroit Cougars, the New York Americans and the New York Rangers joined the Montreal Canadiens and the Toronto Maple Leafs as the six teams in the Stanley Cup playoffs.

5. Name the first American-born player to score fifty goals in an NHL season.

Bobby Carpenter, who was born in Beverly, Massachusetts, recorded fifty-three goals as a member of the Washington Capitals in 1984-85.

6. Name the star goaltenders of the gold medal-winning Olympic teams in 1960 and 1980.

Jack McCartan provided outstanding goaltending for the 1960 gold medal-winning American team. McCartan played in a total of twelve games with the New York Rangers following the Olympics before embarking on a lengthy career in the minor professional leagues. Jim Craig was in goal for the 1980 gold medalists. Craig also had a brief NHL career following the Olympics, seeing action in a total of thirty NHL games with the Atlanta Flames, the Boston Bruins and the Minnesota North Stars.

7. Name the two coaches of Team USA at the 1980 Olympics.

The head coach was Herb Brooks and his assistant was Craig Patrick. Brooks went on to coach in the NHL in seven different seasons with the New York Rangers, the Minnesota North Stars, the New Jersey Devils and the Pittsburgh Penguins. He was also the coach of Team USA at the 2002 Olympic Games. Craig Patrick served as both general manager and coach at various times with the New York Rangers and the Pittsburgh Penguins. He has been general manager of the Pittsburgh Penguins since December of 1989.

8. Name the four women who led the 1998 gold medal-winning Olympic team with eight points each.

Leading Scorers, Team USA, 1998 Olympics

Player	GP	G	A	PTS
Karyn Bye	6	5	3	8
Cammi Granato	6	4	4	8
Katie King	6	4	4	8
Gretchen Ulion	6	3	5	8

9. Who was the leading scorer on the American men's team at the 2002 Winter Olympics?

Brett Hull recorded three goals and five assists for eight points in six games played at the 2002 Olympic tournament.

10. Name the first American-based junior team to win the Memorial Cup.

The Portland Winter Hawks defeated the Oshawa Generals in the 1983 Memorial Cup final to become the first American-based team to win the trophy. The Memorial Cup is the championship trophy for Canadian junior hockey. Several players from that Memorial Cup-winning team went on to play in the NHL. Cam Neely, Ray Ferraro, Brian Curran, John Kordic, and goaltender Mike Vernon who was borrowed from the Calgary Wranglers for the Memorial Cup tournament, all had significant professional careers.

11. Name the father and son who have each played on a gold medal-winning Olympic team for the United States.

Bill Christian skated with the United States Olympic hockey team which won the gold medal at Squaw Valley, California, in 1960. Bill's son, Dave, played on the 1980 gold medal-winning team at the Olympic Games in Lake Placid, New York.

12. Name the five American players who have been the leading scorer at a World Junior Hockey Championship.

American Leading Scorers at a World Junior Championship				
Year	*Player*	*G*	*A*	*PTS*
1989	Jeremy Roenick	8	8	16
1991	Doug Weight	5	14	19
1997	Mike York	5	5	10
1998	Jeff Farkas	6	4	10
1999	Brian Gionta	6	5	11

13. Who was the leading scorer for Team USA in the 1976 Canada Cup?

Robbie Ftorek recorded three goals and two assists for five points in the five games played by Team USA in the 1976 Canada Cup. He was in the midst of a five-year stretch playing in the WHA at the time. Ftorek also played in four of Team USA's six games in the 1981 Canada Cup, where he was held pointless. He saw action in a total of eight NHL seasons on either side of his WHA career. Ftorek went on to coach the Los Angeles Kings, the New Jersey Devils and, most recently, the Boston Bruins in the National Hockey League.

14. Name the American-born player who has played in the most NHL games through the end of the 2002-03 season.

Phil Housley has seen action in a total of 1580 NHL games, which includes 85 playoff games, over his 21 seasons of play in the league through the end of the 2002-03 season.

15. Name the first American-born NHLer to be inducted as a player into the Hockey Hall of Fame.

Goaltender Frank Brimsek was inducted into the Hockey Hall of Fame in 1966. Brimsek was a native of Eveleth, Minnesota, who became an immediate star with the Bruins in 1938-39. He won both the Vezina Trophy and the Calder Trophy as his goaltending took the Bruins to a Stanley Cup. He gained the nickname of "Mr. Zero" when he recorded six shutouts in his first ten NHL games. Brimsek played in a total of nine seasons with the Bruins, on either side of a couple of seasons missed due to military service. He played his final NHL season of 1949-50 with the Chicago Black Hawks.

16. Who were the oldest two players on the United States Olympic hockey team in 1980?

The oldest two players were captain Mike Eruzione and Buzz Schneider. Both Eruzione and Schneider were twenty-five years old in 1980. The other eighteen players on this team ranged in age from eighteen to twenty-two.

17. Name the only Winter Olympics in which the United States did not compete in men's hockey.

No men's hockey team from the United States participated in the 1928 Winter Olympic Games held in St. Moritz, Switzerland.

18. Who was the first American-born player to lead the NHL in goal scoring in a single season?

Keith Tkachuk, who was born in Melrose, Massachusetts, scored fifty-two goals as a Phoenix Coyote in 1996-97.

19. Name the Team USA goaltender who recorded a shutout in his only appearance in the 2002 Olympics.

Mike Dunham recorded a shutout in the Americans' opening game, a 6-0 victory over Finland, on February 15, 2002. Mike Richter and Tom Barrasso also played a single game each in the preliminary round. Richter was the only one of the three to see playoff action at the 2002 Olympics.

20. Team USA compiled a record of six wins and one tie during the "Miracle on Ice" gold medal win at the 1980 Olympics. Which team was able to hold the Americans to a tie at this event?

Sweden and the United States tied 2-2 in the opening game of the tournament for both countries on February 12, 1980. American defenseman Bill Baker tied the game by scoring on Swedish goaltender Pelle Lindbergh with 27 seconds left in the game. Team USA went on to defeat Czechoslovakia, Norway, Romania, West Germany, the Soviet Union and Finland to capture the gold medal in hockey at the 1980 Olympic Winter Games.

THIRD PERIOD - INTERNATIONAL EVENTS

1. Name the last goal scorer for the Soviets in the 1972 Summit Series.

Valeri Vasiliev scored late in the second period to give the Soviets a 5-3 lead in the eighth game of the series. Third period goals by Phil Esposito, Yvan Cournoyer and Paul Henderson resulted in Team Canada's 6-5 win in the decisive match.

2. Name the only two players to score on Czech goalie Dominik Hasek during the 1998 Olympic playoff round.

Mike Modano of Team USA scored on Hasek in a 4-1 loss to the Czech Republic in the quarter-final. Trevor Linden scored for Canada to tie the semi-final game at 1-1 with the Czechs with just over a minute left in regulation time. Hasek blanked the Canadians in the ten minute overtime period and stopped all five players in a shootout as the Czechs took the semi-final 2-1. Hasek led the Czech Republic to a 1-0 win over Russia in the gold medal game.

3. Name the three goalies who have been the MVP of a Canada/World Cup tournament.

Goaltenders have been the MVP at three of the first six Canada/World Cup tournaments. Vladislav Tretiak of the Soviet Union was the first to achieve this honor in 1981. Bill Ranford of Team Canada was the MVP of the 1991 Canada Cup and Mike Richter of the United States was selected as the top player at the first World Cup of Hockey in 1996.

4. Who led the scoring in the 2002 men's Olympic hockey tournament?

Mats Sundin of Sweden recorded five goals and four assists for a tournament-leading nine points while playing in just four games at the 2002 Olympics.

5. Where did Hayley Wickenheiser play professional hockey in 2003?

Canadian Hayley Wickenheiser, often acknowledged as the top female player in the world, moved to men's pro hockey in 2003. She tried out with the Finnish team Kirkkonummi Salamat in January of 2003 and was signed to a contract for the remainder of the season. Wickenheiser played in twenty-three games for this professional men's team, recording two goals and eleven assists. She signed with the team again for the 2003-04 season.

6. Name the only individual to have been the leading scorer in two World Junior Championships.

Vladimir Krutov of the Soviet Union was the leading scorer of both the 1979 World Junior Championship held in Stockholm, Sweden, and the 1980 tournament which was held in Helsinki, Finland.

7. When did the Soviet Union first win a gold medal in hockey at the Olympic Winter Games?

The Soviet Union captured the hockey gold at their first Winter Olympics in 1956 in Cortina, Italy. They compiled a perfect record in seven games to capture the medal. The Soviets had earlier made their debut on the world hockey stage at the 1954 World Championship. The newcomers crushed Canada's representatives, the East York Lyndhursts, 7-2 to win their first world tournament.

8. How many individuals played in both the 1979 Challenge Cup and Rendez-Vous '87? Each tournament featured the NHL All-Stars and the Soviet Nationals.

There were five individuals who played in both of these historic series, all of them members of the Soviet team: Vasili Pervukhin, Mikhail Varnakov, Sergei Starikov, Zinetula Bilyaletdinov and Sergei Makarov. A sixth Soviet, Alexei Kasatonov, was a member of the 1979 Team, but did not play in the series and only saw action in Rendez-Vous '87. The 1987 NHL All-Stars had no returnees from the 1979 Challenge Cup. Mike Bossy, who had played on the 1979 All-Stars, was also chosen to play in Rendez-Vous '87, but was unable to suit up with the NHL All-Stars due to injury.

9. How many countries have won the gold medal at a World Junior Hockey Championship?

Five countries have won a World Junior Hockey Championship in the first twenty-seven years of the tournament, between 1977 and 2003. The Russians, who formerly competed as the Commonwealth of Independent States and earlier as the Soviet Union, have won a total of twelve tournaments. Canada has captured ten titles, while the Czech Republic and Finland have both won the event twice. Sweden has been the World Junior Hockey champion on one occasion.

10. Which four teams scored the most goals in the 2002 men's Olympic hockey tournament?

Canada, the United States, Russia and Latvia were the highest scoring teams at this event. The Canadians, the Americans and the Russians, who took gold, silver and bronze, recorded 22, 26 and 20 goals respectively. Latvia also managed to score 20 goals while playing just four games. Latvia defeated the Ukraine 9-2 in the game to determine ninth place in the tournament.

11. Which country had all three leading scorers at the 2003 men's World Championship?

The three leading scorers of the 2003 World Championship all came from the bronze medal-winning team from Slovakia.

Leading Scorers - 2003 World Championship

Player	Team	GP	G	A	PTS
Ziggy Palffy	Slovakia	9	7	8	15
Jozef Stumpel	Slovakia	9	4	11	15
Lubomir Visnovsky	Slovakia	9	4	8	12

12. Name the goaltender who was selected to the All-Star Team five times at World Championships during the 1970s.

Jiri Holecek of Czechoslovakia was frequently chosen as the top goaltender in international events around the time that Canada was discovering Vladislav Tretiak of the Soviet Union. Holecek was selected ahead of Tretiak as the All-Star goaltender at several World Championships. Holecek received this honor at the tournaments held in 1971, 1972, 1973, 1976 and 1978. Tretiak was selected as the All-Star goalie of the World Championships that took place in 1975, 1979 and 1983.

13. Name the three individuals who were recognized as MVPs of the Rendez-Vous '87 series between the Soviet Nationals and the NHL All-Stars.

Mark Messier was recognized as MVP of the NHL All-Stars while Sergei Makarov was selected as MVP of the Soviet national team. NHL All-Star Wayne Gretzky was chosen as MVP of the two-game tournament.

14. How many major penalties were assigned in the 1972 Summit Series?

There were five major penalties, which were all handed out in the last three games, as the series heated up near the end of this emotional battle. Phil Esposito was the first to receive a five minute major, when his high stick cut Alexander Ragulin near the end of the second period in game six. Gary Bergman and Boris Mikhailov both received majors when a scuffle between the two progressed to the point of kicking near the end of game seven. Team Canada's Rod Gilbert and the Soviets' Evgeny Mishakov both were assessed major penalties at the beginning of the third period of game eight for fighting. While fighting should have resulted in removal from the game, both players served five minutes in the penalty box and were allowed to resume play in the game. The fight was uncharacteristic of the way Gilbert played in the NHL, but he came to be known as "Mad Dog" during the Summit Series as a result of his aggressive play.

15. Who were the head coaches for the 1974 hockey series between Team Canada, represented by WHA players, and the Soviet Union?

Billy Harris, who was head coach of the Toronto Toros of the WHA, led Team Canada '74 while Boris Kulagin was behind the bench for the Soviets. Kulagin had been an assistant to coach Vsevolod Bobrov during the 1972 Summit Series.

16. Name the two future Hall of Famers who represented different countries in the 1984 Canada Cup than the national teams they played for in their initial Canada Cup tournament.

While both participated in their second Canada Cup tournament in 1984, Peter Stastny and Bryan Trottier each played for a different country than in their initial Canada Cup appearance. Stastny had played in the 1976 Canada Cup as a member of the Czechoslovakian team, but participated on Team Canada in the 1984 event. Bryan Trottier had been a member of Team Canada in the 1981 Canada Cup, but took to the ice as a member of Team USA in 1984.

17. Name the four players who saw game action with the Toronto Maple Leafs in 2002-03 and also suited up for Sweden when they faced Canada in the final game of the 2003 World Championship.

Mats Sundin, Mikael Renberg, Jonas Hoglund and goaltender Mikael Tellqvist all played for Sweden in their 3-2 overtime loss against Canada in the gold medal game of the 2003 World Championship.

18. Who were the goalies for Team Canada and the Soviets in Rendez-Vous '87?

Evgeny Belosheikin tended goal for the Soviet Union in the Rendez-Vous '87 series. He had seven of fifty-eight shots beat him in the two games. Grant Fuhr let in eight goals on fifty-three Soviet shots over the series.

19. Name the All-Star Team from the 2003 World Junior Championship which was held in Halifax, Canada.

2003 World Junior All-Star Team

Position	Player	Country
Goal	Marc-Andre Fleury	Canada
Defense	Carlo Colaiacovo	Canada
Defense	Joni Pitkanen	Finland
Forward	Igor Grigorenko	Russia
Forward	Yuri Turbachev	Russia
Forward	Scottie Upshall	Canada

20. Name the only three individuals who have won an Olympic gold medal and a Stanley Cup during the same season.

Ken Morrow, the first to accomplish this, was a member of the United States "Miracle on Ice" team of the 1980 Winter Olympics. Following the Olympics, Morrow joined the New York Islanders and was a member of their first Stanley Cup-winning team. The most recent two players to achieve this were Steve Yzerman and Brendan Shanahan. They were teammates on the Canadian gold medal-winning team at the 2002 Olympics in Salt Lake City and the Detroit Red Wings who captured the Cup later that season.

Mike Richter and Wayne Gretzky were two of the many NHL stars that played in the 1996 World Cup of Hockey.

PHOTO REPLAY

1. How many times did Canada and the United States play each other in the 1996 World Cup?

The two teams faced off on four occasions during the 1996 World Cup. While the Americans had a record of seven losses and a single tie in their previous Canada Cup meetings with the Canadians, they managed to turn the tables in this tournament. Team USA defeated Canada 5-3 in a round-robin match on August 31, 1996, which was played in Philadelphia. The best-of-three final series began in Philadelphia on September 10, with Canada taking the first game in overtime by a score of 4-3. Games two and three were played on September 12 and 14 at the Montreal Forum. The States tied the series and then won the deciding game, both by scores of 5-2.

2. Did Wayne Gretzky score on Mike Richter during these four games?

Gretzky picked up four of his seven points in the games against the Americans. Gretzky recorded two of Canada's three goals against Richter in the losing effort of the round-robin. He didn't record a goal in the last three games, but did pick up an assist in both the first and last games of the final.

3. What goalie, other than Richter, tended net for Team USA in the 1996 World Cup?

Guy Hebert of the Anaheim Mighty Ducks was in goal for a single tournament game, a 9-3 win over Slovakia in round-robin play. Richter was the goaltender in the other six games for Team USA. Goalie Jim Carey of the Washington Capitals, who was the third netminder on the Team USA roster, did not play in the tournament.

4. Who did the Canadians and the Americans defeat in the 1996 World Cup semi-final games?

Team Canada defeated Sweden 3-2 in double overtime in a semi-final match played in Philadelphia on September 7. Team USA advanced to the final with a 5-2 win over Russia on September 8, in a game held in Ottawa.

The Big League

The National Hockey League began in 1917-18 with only four teams competing. The NHL rapidly expanded in the 1920s, becoming a league of ten by 1926-27. As a result of the Great Depression and World War II, the number of teams decreased by 1942-43 to what became known as the "Original Six". This era lasted until 1967, when the NHL added six new teams. Additional expansions occurred in 1970, 1972 and 1974, along with the demise of one franchise in 1978. This brought the league to seventeen teams in 1978-79. Four surviving teams from the World Hockey Association entered the NHL as expansion franchises in 1979. Since then, nine new franchises have joined the league between 1991 and 2000. The end result of these many changes is the thirty team National Hockey League as we know it today.

FIRST PERIOD - THE ORIGINAL SIX TEAMS

1. **Name the last player on each of the Original Six franchises to lead the league in points in an NHL season.**

<u>Last Scoring Leader from each Original Six Franchise</u>

Season	Team	Player
1937-38	Toronto Maple Leafs	Gordie Drillon
1941-42	New York Rangers	Bryan Hextall
1962-63	Detroit Red Wings	Gordie Howe
1967-68	Chicago Black Hawks	Stan Mikita
1974-75	Boston Bruins	Bobby Orr
1977-78	Montreal Canadiens	Guy Lafleur

2. Name the three future Hall of Famers who served as captain of the Montreal Canadiens between 1926-27 and 1938-39.

Sylvio Mantha served as captain of the Canadiens for six seasons, from 1926-27 through 1931-32. Goaltender George Hainsworth then served as captain for the single season of 1932-33, before being replaced by Mantha who again wore the "C" for three more seasons. Mantha did not return to the Canadiens for 1936-37 and the captaincy was taken over by Babe Siebert, who was acquired from the Boston Bruins. Siebert remained captain for his final three NHL seasons, before his untimely death in the summer of 1939.

3. Name the only player, other than Gordie Howe, to lead the Detroit Red Wings in scoring during the fourteen seasons between 1950-51 and 1963-64.

Earl "Dutch" Reibel led the Detroit Red Wings in scoring with sixty-six points in 1954-55. Howe finished only four points behind Reibel in second place. This marked the only time in the fourteen seasons between 1950-51 and 1963-64 that Gordie Howe was not the leading scorer for the Red Wings franchise.

4. Name the two individuals who played in twenty-one NHL seasons with the Boston Bruins.

Both Ray Bourque and Johnny Bucyk played in a total of twenty-one NHL seasons with the Boston Bruins. Bucyk arrived by a trade with the Detroit Red Wings in 1957 and played with the Bruins until his retirement in 1978. Ray Bourque began his NHL career with the Bruins in 1979 and was a member of the club until his trade to the Colorado Avalanche in March of 2000. Both Bucyk (#9) and Bourque (#77) have seen their sweater numbers retired by the Bruins to honor their contributions to the franchise.

5. Name the last team to have players win the Lady Byng Trophy in three consecutive NHL seasons.

The Toronto Maple Leafs had a player win the Lady Byng for three consecutive years from 1960-61 through 1962-63. Red Kelly was awarded the trophy in the first of these seasons, while Dave Keon won back-to-back trophies for the next two years.

6. Name the three future Hall of Famers who began playing with the Chicago Black Hawks in 1957-58.

Bobby Hull, Glenn Hall and Ted Lindsay all skated with the Chicago Black Hawks for the first time in 1957-58. Bobby Hull was in his rookie season, while Glenn Hall and Ted Lindsay arrived from the Detroit Red Wings in a trade.

7. Who was the last member of the New York Rangers to be an NHL First All-Star in three consecutive seasons?

Bryan Hextall of the New York Rangers was selected as the right winger of the First All-Star Team for three seasons from 1939-40 through 1941-42. Hextall had an outstanding career with the Rangers from 1936-37 through 1947-48. He was inducted into the Hockey Hall of Fame in 1969. His sons Bryan Jr. and Denis went on to play in the NHL, as did his grandson, goaltender Ron Hextall.

8. Name the only Original Six franchise that the Detroit Red Wings have not defeated in a Stanley Cup final to capture the Cup.

The Red Wings have never defeated the Chicago Blackhawks in a Stanley Cup final. The Blackhawks have won only three Cups in their history, but two of those were in a final series against Detroit in 1934 and again in 1961.

Detroit Red Wing Stanley Cup Championships vs. Original Six Teams

Year	Opponent	Series
1936	Toronto Maple Leafs	3-1
1937	New York Rangers	3-2
1943	Boston Bruins	4-0
1950	New York Rangers	4-3
1952	Montreal Canadiens	4-0
1954	Montreal Canadiens	4-3
1955	Montreal Canadiens	4-3

9. Name the four Calder Trophy winners who went on to be members of all four Montreal Stanley Cup-winning teams between 1965 and 1969.

Lorne "Gump" Worsley won the Calder Trophy as a member of the New York Rangers in 1953. Ralph Backstrom received the honor in 1959, Bobby Rousseau in 1962 and Jacques Laperriere in 1964. These three players all won the Calder as members of the Montreal Canadiens. All four were teammates on the Stanley Cup winners in 1965, 1966, 1968 and 1969.

10. Name the two teams that prevented Toronto from winning a fourth consecutive Stanley Cup.

The Detroit Red Wings were the first to do this when Leo Reise scored at 8:39 of overtime to give the Red Wings a 1-0 win in the seventh and deciding game of the 1950 semi-final. The Maple Leafs had been Cup winners in 1947, 1948 and 1949. The Montreal Canadiens were the only other team to prevent four consecutive Leaf Cup wins, as Toronto entered the 1965 playoffs as Cup winners in the three previous seasons. Montreal's Claude Provost scored at 16:33 of overtime in the sixth game of the 1965 semi-final. His goal knocked the Leafs out of the playoffs as the Canadiens advanced to the Stanley Cup final.

11. Which was the last of the Original Six franchises to have a player first record fifty goals in a single NHL season?

The Toronto Maple Leafs did not have a fifty-goal scorer until Rick Vaive hit this mark on March 24, 1982. Vaive went on to score fifty-four goals that season and followed it up with fifty-one and fifty-two in the next two seasons.

First Fifty-Goal Seasons for Players on each Original Six Franchise

Team	Player	Season
Montreal Canadiens	Maurice Richard	1944-45
Chicago Black Hawks	Bobby Hull	1961-62
Boston Bruins	Phil Esposito, Johnny Bucyk	1970-71
New York Rangers	Vic Hadfield	1971-72
Detroit Red Wings	Mickey Redmond	1972-73
Toronto Maple Leafs	Rick Vaive	1981-82

12. Name the player who was a member of the last Stanley Cup-winning team with both the Boston Bruins and the Toronto Maple Leafs.

Mike Walton was a member of both the 1966-67 Toronto Maple Leafs and the 1971-72 Boston Bruins.

13. Name the last four players to win the Stanley Cup as both a Montreal Canadien and a Toronto Maple Leaf.

Player	Montreal Cup Wins	Toronto Cup Wins
Frank Mahovlich	1971, 1973	1962, 1963, 1964, 1967
Dick Duff	1965, 1966, 1968, 1969	1962, 1963
Larry Hillman	1969	1964, 1967
Bert Olmstead	1953, 1956, 1957, 1958	1962

14. How many times did a team reach one hundred points in a single NHL season prior to expansion in 1967?

This only happened on three occasions. The 1950-51 and 1951-52 Detroit Red Wings recorded 101 and 100 points respectively. The Montreal Canadiens also reached 100 points in the 1955-56 season.

15. Name the first three players to score fifty goals in an NHL season as a member of the Detroit Red Wings.

Mickey Redmond hit the fifty-goal mark in two consecutive seasons. He scored fifty-two goals in 1972-73 and followed it up with fifty-one in 1973-74. Danny Grant scored fifty goals as a Red Wing in the 1974-75 season. The third Red Wing to reach this milestone was John Ogrodnick when he recorded fifty-five goals ten years later in the 1984-85 season.

16. Which Original Six franchise has had the most winners of the Calder Trophy?

The Toronto Maple Leafs have had nine rookies awarded the Calder Trophy in their history. The New York Rangers are close behind having had eight winners.

Toronto Calder Trophy Winners

Season	Player
1936-37	Syl Apps
1942-43	Gaye Stewart
1943-44	Gus Bodnar
1944-45	Frank McCool
1946-47	Howie Meeker
1957-58	Frank Mahovlich
1960-61	Dave Keon
1962-63	Kent Douglas
1965-66	Brit Selby

17. Name the first four pairs of brothers to have played together for the Toronto Maple Leafs in the same season.

The first were Art and Harvey "Busher" Jackson. Younger brother Art joined Busher during the three seasons of 1934-35 through 1936-37. Nick Metz suited up with younger brother Don during the 1939 playoffs. They were gone for military duty between 1942 and 1944, but the Metz brothers again played together on the Leafs from 1944-45 through 1947-48 when Nick retired. They are the only brothers to have been together on Maple Leaf Cup-winning clubs as they shared the Cup four times between 1942 and 1948. Barry and Brian Cullen both saw action with the Toronto Maple Leafs in the four seasons between 1955-56 and 1958-59. Miroslav and Peter Ihnacak are the most recent brothers to have skated together as Maple Leafs, which they did during the 1985-86 and 1986-87 seasons.

18. Name the only two Original Six match-ups that have never happened in a Stanley Cup final series.

The Chicago Blackhawks have never faced either the Boston Bruins or the New York Rangers in a Stanley Cup final series.

19. Who received the last penalty of the Original Six era?

Jim Pappin of the Toronto Maple Leafs received a penalty for slashing at 11:46 of the third period in the sixth and final game of the 1967 Stanley Cup final. Pappin's penalty was the only one assigned in this final period of hockey in the Original Six era.

20. Name the only captain of a 1966-67 NHL franchise who did not go on to become a member of the Hockey Hall of Fame.

Bob Nevin was captain of the New York Rangers in the 1966-67 season. The other five captains who were all later inducted into the Hockey Hall of Fame were: George Armstrong (Toronto), Jean Beliveau (Montreal), John Bucyk (Boston), Alex Delvecchio (Detroit) and Pierre Pilote (Chicago).

SECOND PERIOD
THE NEXT ELEVEN SURVIVING FRANCHISES

1. Name the four former Cup winners with Montreal who faced the Canadiens in both the 1968 and 1969 Stanley Cup finals as members of the St. Louis Blues.

Gordon "Red" Berenson, Noel Picard, Jim Roberts and Jean-Guy Talbot were all members of the St. Louis Blues who faced the Montreal Canadiens in both the 1968 and 1969 Stanley Cup final series. Doug Harvey and Dickie Moore were former Montreal champions who skated with the Blues in the 1968 final, while former Canadiens Cup winners Jacques Plante and Ab McDonald were members of the Blues for the 1969 Cup final.

2. Which NHL franchise was the first to record a hundred or more points in five consecutive seasons?

The Philadelphia Flyers first accomplished this by recording over one hundred points in the five seasons from 1973-74 through 1977-78. The Montreal Canadiens actually began a run of eight consecutive hundred-point seasons the following year, 1974-75, and the Boston Bruins followed up with five consecutive seasons of one hundred points or more from 1975-76 on. By the end of the 2002-03 season, the Edmonton Oilers, the New Jersey Devils and the Dallas Stars had also achieved this mark.

3. Name the only NHL team to have placed three players on the NHL All-Rookie Team in the same season.

The 1986-87 Los Angeles Kings had three members of their franchise named to the All-Rookie Team for that season.

1986-87 NHL All-Rookie Team

Player	Team	Position
Ron Hextall	Philadelphia Flyers	goal
Steve Duchesne	Los Angeles Kings	defense
Brian Benning	St. Louis Blues	defense
Jimmy Carson	Los Angeles Kings	center
Jim Sandlak	Vancouver Canucks	right wing
Luc Robitaille	Los Angeles Kings	left wing

4. Name the last individual to serve as head coach while still playing with the team.

Charlie Burns took over as head coach while playing with the Minnesota North Stars in December of 1969 and remained in the dual role for the rest of the season. The Stars finished third in the Western Division and were eliminated by the St. Louis Blues in their quarter-final series. Following his retirement as a player, Burns had one more stint as head coach of the North Stars from January through April of 1975.

5. How many times have the Pittsburgh Penguins received the Presidents' Trophy, which is presented to the team with the best overall record in the NHL regular season?

The Pittsburgh Penguins have only been awarded this trophy on a single occasion for their 1992-93 season. The Penguins had previously captured the Stanley Cup in both 1991 and 1992. However, after achieving the best overall record in the NHL, they were eliminated by the New York Islanders in the 1993 playoffs.

6. When did the Vancouver Canucks win their first NHL playoff series?

The Canucks didn't win a playoff series until 1982, when they won three in a row to advance all the way to the Stanley Cup final. Vancouver had missed the playoffs in six of their first eleven seasons and were eliminated in the first round in the other five years. However, in 1982, the Canucks swept the Calgary Flames in the Smythe Division semi-final; defeated the Los Angeles Kings in the division final; and eliminated the Chicago Black Hawks in the Western Conference final. The Vancouver Canucks lost to the New York Islanders in the 1982 Stanley Cup final.

7. Name the four goaltenders who have won the Vezina Trophy as members of the Buffalo Sabres.

Goaltending partners Don Edwards and Bob Sauve of the 1979-80 Buffalo Sabres were the first to accomplish this. Tom Barrasso won his only Vezina in his rookie season of 1983-84, while Dominik Hasek won the Trophy on six occasions with the Sabres, the first being in 1993-94 and his last in 2000-01.

8. Name the two NHL franchises that have not broken their single season point record attained in 1974-75, through the end of the 2002-03 season.

Both the Buffalo Sabres and the Los Angeles Kings hit franchise high totals for points in 1974-75. Neither franchise has been able to reach these lofty heights again. In 1974-75, Buffalo finished first in the Adams Division with a 49-16-15 record for 113 points. The Sabres lost the Stanley Cup final to the Philadelphia Flyers that season. That same year, the Los Angeles Kings finished second in the Norris Division with a 42-17-21 record for 105 points. They were eliminated in the preliminary round by the Toronto Maple Leafs.

9. Name the four players to have won the Calder Trophy as members of the New York Islanders.

Player	Season
Denis Potvin	1973-74
Bryan Trottier	1975-76
Mike Bossy	1977-78
Bryan Berard	1996-97

10. How many players have won the Calder Trophy with the Flames franchise?

Five players from this franchise have been named the outstanding rookie. Eric Vail and Willi Plett were Calder winners in 1975 and 1977, when the team was in Atlanta. Gary Suter, Joe Nieuwendyk and Sergei Makarov all won the Calder Trophy as rookie of the year with the Calgary Flames, in 1986, 1988 and 1990 respectively.

11. Which team has the worst winning percentage for one season in NHL history?

The Washington Capitals recorded an all-time low in 1974-75. The Capitals had an 8-67-5 record for twenty-one points in eighty games. This .131 winning percentage is the worst ever in NHL history. The 1992-93 Ottawa Senators and San Jose Sharks, both with .143 winning percentages, are the only teams in recent history to take a run at the record of the 1974-75 Washington Capitals.

12. Who was the first captain of the New Jersey Devils?

Don Lever was the captain of the New Jersey Devils for the 1982-83 season.

13. Which NHL team made their twenty-fourth consecutive playoff appearance in 2003?

The St. Louis Blues appeared in their twenty-fourth consecutive playoffs in 2003. The all-time record is held by the Boston Bruins who made twenty-nine consecutive playoff appearances between 1968 and 1996.

14. Name the first NHL team to win fifteen games in a playoff year and still not capture the Stanley Cup.

The 1987 Philadelphia Flyers were the first team to win fifteen games, but not the Stanley Cup, in one year. The first round of the playoffs was increased from a best-of-five to a best-of-seven series in 1987. Therefore, to advance all the way to the seventh game of a Stanley Cup final, a team now required fifteen wins. The Edmonton Oilers defeated Philadelphia in a seven-game final to take the Cup in 1987. The 1994 Vancouver Canucks, the 2001 New Jersey Devils and the 2003 Anaheim Mighty Ducks have all recorded fifteen wins in a playoff year, without a Stanley Cup victory.

15. What is the longest stretch of time that the New York Islanders have missed the playoffs?

The Islanders missed the playoffs for seven consecutive seasons between 1994-95 and 2000-01. In their first twenty-two seasons, between 1972-73 and 1993-94, the Islanders had only missed the playoffs in a total of five years.

16. Who was the first Buffalo Sabre selected as a member of the NHL First All-Star Team?

Rick Martin of the Buffalo Sabres was selected as the NHL First All-Star Team left winger in both 1973-74 and 1974-75.

17. Which NHL franchise did not make the playoffs until their ninth season in the National Hockey League?

The Washington Capitals, who entered the NHL in 1974-75, did not make the playoffs until 1983. In their first playoff year, they met up with the eventual Stanley Cup champion, the New York Islanders, who defeated the Capitals three games to one in a best-of-five Patrick Division semi-final. This year marked a turning point, however, as the Capitals then managed to make the playoffs for a total of fourteen consecutive seasons between 1983 and 1996.

18. What is the highest point total ever recorded by a New Jersey Devil in a single NHL season?

Patrik Elias scored forty goals and picked up fifty-six assists for ninety-six points in the 2000-01 season.

19. Name the only three general managers over the first thirty-one NHL seasons of the New York Islanders.

Bill Torrey, Don Maloney and Mike Milbury have all been the general manager of the New York Islanders. Bill Torrey served as general manager for the first twenty years of the franchise from 1972-73 to the end of the 1991-92 season. Don Maloney then assumed general manager duties until he was replaced by Mike Milbury in December of 1995. Milbury was still general manager of the team in 2003.

20. Name the first expansion team to face all of the Original Six franchises in playoff competition.

The St. Louis Blues were the first franchise to match up against each of the Original Six in the playoffs.

First St. Louis Playoff Series Vs Original Six Teams

Year	Series	Opponents	Result (Winner)
1968	final	Montreal Canadiens	4-0 (Montreal)
1970	final	Boston Bruins	4-0 (Boston)
1973	quarter-final	Chicago Black Hawks	4-1 (Chicago)
1981	quarter-final	New York Rangers	4-2 (New York)
1984	division semi-final	Detroit Red Wings	3-1 (St. Louis)
1986	division final	Toronto Maple Leafs	4-3 (St. Louis)

THIRD PERIOD
THIRTEEN MAKEƑ IT THIRTY

1. Name the coaches of the four new NHL franchises in 1979-80.

The Edmonton Oilers, the Hartford Whalers, the Quebec Nordiques and the Winnipeg Jets all joined the NHL as WHA survivors in 1979. The Oilers were coached by Glen Sather; the Whalers by Don Blackburn; the Nordiques by Jacques Demers; and the Winnipeg Jets by both Tom McVie and Bill Sutherland.

2. Name the individual who played in the most NHL seasons as a member of the Edmonton Oilers.

Kevin Lowe played in fifteen NHL seasons as a member of the Edmonton Oilers. His first thirteen seasons in the league, from 1979-80 through 1991-92, were with the Oilers. He was then traded to the New York Rangers in 1992, where he played for four seasons before again signing with Edmonton as a free agent in September of 1996. He saw action in both 1996-97 and 1997-98 before retiring from the NHL as a player. Kevin Lowe became an assistant coach with the Oilers in 1998 and was named head coach in 1999. He assumed the role of general manager in June of 2000.

3. Name the two members of the Quebec Nordiques to be awarded the Calder Trophy.

Peter Stastny was awarded the Calder for the 1980-81 season. Peter Forsberg received the honor in 1995, just prior to the Nordiques' move to Colorado.

4. Name the last team to face three Original Six opponents in the same playoff year.

In the 2002 Stanley Cup playoffs, the Carolina Hurricanes eliminated the Montreal Canadiens in the Eastern Conference semi-final; defeated the Toronto Maple Leafs in the Conference final; and ultimately lost to the Detroit Red Wings in the Stanley Cup final series.

5. Name the four individuals who have served as a general manager of the Coyotes since the arrival of the franchise to Phoenix in 1996.

John Paddock, Bobby Smith, Cliff Fletcher and Mike Barnett have all served as general manager of the Coyotes at various times since the franchise's arrival from Winnipeg in 1996 through to the end of the 2002-03 season. Bobby Smith had the longest tenure as general manager to date, taking over the responsibilities on December 11, 1996 and continuing in that capacity until February 17, 2001.

6. Which NHL team has shown the biggest improvement in points from one season to the next?

The 1993-94 San Jose Sharks showed a fifty-eight point improvement over their previous season. The 1992-93 San Jose Sharks had gone 11-71-2 for twenty-four points. The following season, the Sharks improved to 33-35-16 for eighty-two points. That year, San Jose defeated Detroit in seven games in the Western Conference quarter-final before being eliminated by the Toronto Maple Leafs in game seven of the Conference semi-final.

7. Name the only player to have skated with the Ottawa Senators in both their first season of 1992-93 and their most recent season of 2002-03.

Jody Hull skated with the Ottawa Senators in their first season of 1992-93, when he recorded thirty-four points in sixty-nine games. He previously had played for both Hartford and the New York Rangers and moved on to play for Florida, Tampa Bay and Philadelphia before coming back to Ottawa as a free agent in January of 2002. The defensive right winger recorded eleven points in seventy games with the Senators in 2002-03.

8. Name the two individuals who were the head coach of a Stanley Cup-winning team prior to becoming the head coach of the Tampa Bay Lightning.

Terry Crisp was a Stanley Cup champion as head coach of the 1989 Calgary Flames. He also served as Tampa Bay's head coach from 1992-93 into the 1997-98 season. Jacques Demers became head coach of the Tampa Bay Lightning in 1997-98 and served in that capacity through the end of the 1998-99 season. Demers had previously coached the Stanley Cup-winning Montreal Canadiens in 1993.

9. How many team members of the Anaheim Mighty Ducks had previously won a Stanley Cup when they entered the 2003 Cup final?

There were three players on this team who had previously won the Stanley Cup. Petr Sykora had been a member of the 2000 New Jersey Devils; Sandis Ozolinsh played with the 1996 Colorado Avalanche; and Fredrik Olausson skated with the 2002 Detroit Red Wings.

10. How many times have the Florida Panthers made the playoffs in their first ten NHL seasons?

The Florida Panthers have only qualified for the Stanley Cup playoffs on three occasions during their first ten NHL seasons, from 1993-94 through 2002-03. Success seemed to come early to the franchise as they missed the playoffs by only a single point in their inaugural season of 1993-94. In their first playoff appearance in 1996, they actually advanced all the way to the Stanley Cup final, defeating Boston, Philadelphia and Pittsburgh. They were then swept by the Colorado Avalanche. The Panthers only qualified for the playoffs on two other occasions. In 1997, they were defeated by the New York Rangers in the Conference quarter-final. In 2000, they were swept by the New Jersey Devils when they again made the Conference quarter-final.

11. Who scored the first goal as a Nashville Predator?

Andrew Brunette scored for Nashville at 5:12 of the first period against the visiting Carolina Hurricanes on October 13, 1998. This goal got the Predators started en route to a 3-2 win over Carolina. The Predators had been held scoreless in their first game, a 1-0 loss to the Florida Panthers, on October 10, 1998.

12. Name the only three individuals to have coached the Atlanta Thrashers.

Curt Fraser was named head coach for the Atlanta Thrashers for their first season in 1999-2000. Fraser remained at the helm until he was relieved during the 2002-03 season, being replaced by general manager Don Waddell on a short-term basis. The position was quickly handed over to Bob Hartley who had been recently released by the Colorado Avalanche.

13. Who played in the most games for the Columbus Blue Jackets over their first three seasons in the NHL?

David Vyborny played in 233 of the Blue Jackets' 246 games through their first three seasons in the National Hockey League, from 2000-01 through 2002-03.

14. Name the three individuals selected by the Minnesota Wild in the 2000 Expansion Draft who played for the Wild in the 2003 playoffs.

Minnesota selected defenseman Filip Kuba from the Calgary Flames and forwards Jim Dowd from the Edmonton Oilers and Darby Hendrickson from the Vancouver Canucks in the NHL Expansion Draft held in June of 2000. All three players were still members of the club and saw game action in the 2003 Stanley Cup playoffs.

15. Name the only three NHL teams whose nicknames are singular.

The Colorado Avalanche, the Minnesota Wild and the Tampa Bay Lightning are the only three teams in the history of the league to have nicknames that are singular.

16. Who led the Carolina Hurricanes in goal scoring in the last four seasons?

From 1999-2000 through 2002-03, Jeff O'Neill led the Carolina Hurricanes in goal scoring with totals of 25, 41, 31 and 30 goals respectively.

17. How many home games did the Anaheim Mighty Ducks lose in the 2003 playoffs?

The Mighty Ducks had a record of nine wins and one loss at home in their 2003 playoff run. The single home loss came in game three of the Western Conference semi-final when they were defeated 2-1 by the Dallas Stars on April 28.

18. Name the three goalies who played net for the Columbus Blue Jackets in their first three NHL seasons.

Ron Tugnutt played goal for the Blue Jackets in their first two seasons, 2000-01 and 2001-02. Jean-Francois Labbe played a backup role in both 2001-02 and 2002-03. Marc Denis is the only goaltender to have played games in all three of these seasons for the Columbus Blue Jackets.

19. Name the only player to appear in every regular season game over the first three seasons of the Minnesota Wild.

Antti Laaksonen appeared in all 246 regular season games with the Minnesota Wild from their inaugural season of 2000-01 to 2002-03. Laaksonen missed his first games with the Minnesota Wild in the 2003 playoffs when he skated in only sixteen of their eighteen playoff games.

20. Name the two present NHL cities to have never hosted a Stanley Cup playoff game through 2003.

Only Columbus and Nashville have never hosted an NHL playoff game through to the end of the 2003 Stanley Cup playoffs. While the Atlanta Thrashers have never made the playoffs, the previous NHL franchise in Atlanta, the Flames, qualified for the playoffs in six of the eight seasons they played in the city. The Flames relocated to Calgary in 1980.

**The Montreal Canadiens celebrated another
Stanley Cup victory in 1979.**

PHOTO REPLAY

1. In which decade have the Montreal Canadiens won the most Stanley Cups?

The Canadiens' Stanley Cup victory in 1979 marked their sixth of that decade. Of their twenty-four Cup wins, this was the largest number to be recorded in one decade. They won their first Stanley Cup in 1916 as an NHA team. The Habs hoisted the Cup as an NHL team for the first time in 1924. The Canadiens won twice in both the 1930s and the 1940s before recording five Stanley Cup championships in both the 1950s and 1960s. The last two Stanley Cup-winning years for the Montreal Canadiens were in 1986 and 1993.

2. Which was the last of the Original Six franchises to lose a Stanley Cup final to the Canadiens?

The New York Rangers were the last of the Original Six to fall to the Canadiens in a Stanley Cup final. The two clubs first met in a final in 1979. The Canadiens pictured are celebrating a 4-1 victory over the Rangers in the fifth and final game of the series. Montreal first defeated Boston in 1930, Chicago in 1931, Detroit in 1956, and Toronto in 1959 in Stanley Cup final series.

3. When had the Rangers previously played in a Stanley Cup final in the Montreal Forum?

The New York Rangers faced the Montreal Maroons in a best-of-five final series that went the limit in 1928. Rangers' coach Lester Patrick made his famous emergency appearance in the Rangers' net in game two of the series. The Rangers captured their first Cup in this series which saw all five games played at the Montreal Forum.

4. How many times has an NHL team won the Stanley Cup with a different captain in two consecutive years?

This has only happened on two occasions. The first time was in 1948 and 1949 when the Toronto Maple Leafs won consecutive Stanley Cups. Retiring star Syl Apps was the captain of the 1948 Toronto Maple Leafs and was succeeded by Ted Kennedy who led the Leafs to another Stanley Cup championship the following year. A similar situation happened in 1956 and 1957, when the Montreal Canadiens' retiring captain Emile "Butch" Bouchard of the 1956 team, was followed as captain by Maurice "Rocket" Richard on the 1957 squad. It should also be noted that Yvan Cournoyer was the official captain of Montreal's four consecutive championship teams between 1976 and 1979. However, he was injured and unable to play in two of these playoff years. Cournoyer played and wore the "C" in 1976 and 1978, but Serge Savard served as the on-ice captain for the 1977 and 1979 playoffs during Cournoyer's absence.

Leading Roles

Ask any individual on a successful team what makes their organization work and they will undoubtedly list effective leadership. Over the years, there have been numerous coaches, captains and All-Star players who have demonstrated leadership qualities on and off the ice. The ability to inspire by example and motivate others is essential in a leader.

FIRST PERIOD - CAPTAIN, OH MY CAPTAIN

1. Name the captain of each of the Original Six franchises the last time they won the Stanley Cup.

Team	Last Stanley Cup	Captain
Detroit Red Wings	2002	Steve Yzerman
New York Rangers	1994	Mark Messier
Montreal Canadiens	1993	Guy Carbonneau
Boston Bruins	1972	no captain*
Toronto Maple Leafs	1967	George Armstrong
Chicago Black Hawks	1961	Eddie Litzenberger

*Boston had no designated captain between 1967-68 through 1972-73. However, Johnny Bucyk served as the captain both before and after this, and in many ways took on the role of captain of the Bruins during their last Stanley Cup-winning season.

2. Name the first NHL captain to score the Cup-winning goal for his team.

Bill Cook scored the Stanley Cup-winning goal in the 1933 Stanley Cup final. Cook scored at 7:33 of overtime to give the Rangers a 1-0 victory over the Maple Leafs on April 13, 1933. The Rangers won the best-of-five Stanley Cup final series three games to one.

3. When was the last time that the Cup-winning captain was the leading scorer for that playoff season?

Joe Sakic led the playoffs in scoring in 2001 when his Colorado Avalanche won the Cup. Sakic had thirteen goals and thirteen assists for twenty-six points in twenty-one games played. Sakic had also been the playoff scoring leader in 1996 when the Avalanche won their first Stanley Cup.

4. Name the first individual to win a Stanley Cup as an NHL captain and later as a coach.

Eddie Gerard was the captain of the Cup-winning Ottawa Senators in 1920, 1921 and again in 1923. Gerard retired as a player following the 1923 Cup victory, but returned to the league as coach of the expansion Montreal Maroons in 1924. The following season, 1925-26, Gerard was head coach when the Montreal Maroons captured their first Stanley Cup.

5. Who was the highest scoring captain in the 2002-03 NHL season?

Captain Markus Naslund of the Vancouver Canucks finished second overall in the NHL scoring race in 2002-03, with a total of 104 points.

6. Name the three Hall of Fame captains who led the Black Hawks in the five seasons between 1949-50 and 1953-54.

Doug Bentley was the captain for 1949-50 and was followed by Jack Stewart who led the team the following two seasons. Bill Gadsby then held the position for both 1952-53 and 1953-54. Both Doug Bentley and Jack Stewart were inducted into the Hockey Hall of Fame in 1964, while Gadsby received the honor in 1970.

7. Who was the captain of the Stanley Cup-winning Vancouver Millionaires?

Hall of Famer Si Griffis played in eight seasons with the Vancouver Millionaires of the Pacific Coast Hockey Association. He was the captain of the team when they won the Stanley Cup in 1915, although he was unable to play in the series against Ottawa due to injury.

8. Name the only player to have been captain of both the Atlanta Flames and the Pittsburgh Penguins.

Jean Pronovost was named captain of the Pittsburgh Penguins for the 1977-78 season, his tenth with the club. Pronovost was then traded to the Atlanta Flames in September of 1978. He was named captain for 1979-80, which was the last season the Flames spent in Atlanta before they were relocated to Calgary.

9. Who was the first captain of the Tampa Bay Lightning?

Tampa Bay did not appoint a captain for their first three seasons in the NHL. Paul Ysebaert was traded to the Lightning in February of 1995, and was named their captain for the following season, 1995-96.

10. Name the only two individuals to have served as captain of the Phoenix Coyotes to the end of the 2002-03 season.

Keith Tkachuk served as captain from the franchise's arrival in Phoenix in 1996 until he was traded to St. Louis in March of 2001. Teppo Numminen was captain from the beginning of the 2001-02 season until he was dealt to Dallas in July of 2003.

11. Name the two former captains of the New York Islanders who have been inducted into the Hockey Hall of Fame.

Both Clark Gillies and Denis Potvin served as captain with the New York Islanders and went on to be inducted into the Hockey Hall of Fame. Gillies took over the captaincy from Ed Westfall in the 1976-77 season and remained in that role through 1979. Potvin then became captain and served in that capacity through the next eight seasons. Potvin was inducted into the Hockey Hall of Fame in 1991, while Gillies followed in 2002.

12. Who was the longest serving captain of the Hartford Whalers?

Ron Francis took over from Mark Johnson as Whalers' captain in 1984-85 and continued in that role until his trade to Pittsburgh in 1991. Francis returned to the franchise when they relocated to Carolina. He was again appointed captain in 1999-2000 and was still serving as the Hurricanes' captain at the end of the 2002-03 season.

13. Who did Steve Yzerman succeed as captain of the Detroit Red Wings?

Danny Gare served as the captain of the Detroit Red Wings for four seasons from 1982-83 through 1985-86. Gare moved to the Edmonton Oilers as a free agent in 1986, with Yzerman becoming captain for the 1986-87 season. Yzerman is now the longest serving captain with a single NHL team.

14. Name the individual who has the distinction of captaining a losing NHL team in the most Stanley Cup finals.

Hall of Famer Emile "Butch" Bouchard captained the Montreal Canadiens for eight seasons, from 1948-49 through 1955-56. While the Canadiens won two Stanley Cups under Bouchard's captaincy in 1953 and 1956, they were also on the losing end in four Stanley Cup finals. Toronto defeated them in 1951 and they lost to Detroit in 1952, 1954 and 1955.

15. How many general managers of NHL clubs, heading into the 2003-04 NHL season, used to be the captain of that same club?

There were five general managers heading in the 2003-04 NHL season who each served as a captain of their club. Bob Clarke (Philadelphia), Bob Gainey (Montreal), Kevin Lowe (Edmonton), Dave Taylor (Los Angeles) and Doug Wilson (San Jose) all served as captains of these NHL clubs in the past.

16. Name the three individuals who served as both a captain and a coach of the Buffalo Sabres.

Floyd Smith served as the Sabres' first captain in 1970-71. Smith went on to coach for a single game with the Sabres in 1971-72 and later held the position for three full seasons, from 1974-75 through 1976-77. Jim Schoenfeld captained the team from 1974-75 through the end of the 1976-77 season. Schoenfeld was then behind the bench as head coach for forty-three games with the Sabres in 1985-86. Lindy Ruff took over the captaincy from Gilbert Perreault in November of 1986 and remained the Sabres' captain until March of 1989. Ruff was appointed head coach of the Buffalo Sabres in 1997.

17. How many former NHL captains skated with the 2002-03 Toronto Maple Leafs?

Leaf captain Mats Sundin had seven former NHL captains join him on the Maple Leafs during the 2002-03 season.

Former Captains	Team	Year(s)
Shayne Corson	Edmonton Oilers	1994-95
	St. Louis Blues	1995-96
Tom Fitzgerald	Nashville Predators	1998-99 to 2001-02
Doug Gilmour	Toronto Maple Leafs	1994-95 to 1996-97
	Chicago Blackhawks	1999-2000
Alexander Mogilny	Buffalo Sabres	1993-94
Bryan McCabe	New York Islanders	1997-98
Owen Nolan	San Jose Sharks	1998-99 to 2002-03
Mikael Renberg	Tampa Bay Lightning	1997-98

18. Name the two individuals to have captained both the Carolina Hurricanes and the Philadelphia Flyers.

Kevin Dineen and Keith Primeau have served as captains of both of these franchises. Kevin Dineen served as captain of the 1993-94 Philadelphia Flyers. He was traded to Hartford in 1995, and was appointed captain of the Whalers for their last year in Hartford in 1996-97. He remained captain for the franchise's first year in Carolina in 1997-98. Keith Primeau succeeded Dineen as Carolina's captain for the 1998-99 season. Primeau chose not to return to the Hurricanes in 1999-2000 and was eventually traded to Philadelphia in January of that season. He took over the Flyers' captaincy from Eric Desjardins during the 2001-02 season, a position he still held at the end of the 2003 playoffs.

19. Who was the last captain of the Minnesota North Stars?

Mark Tinordi served as captain for the last two seasons that the North Stars were in Minnesota. He was also the captain for the first season after the Stars had relocated to Dallas for 1993-94.

20. Name the six individuals who served as a captain over the first twenty NHL seasons of the Vancouver Canucks.

Andre Boudrias, Orland Kurtenbach, Don Lever, Kevin McCarthy, Chris Oddleifson and Stan Smyl all served as a captain of the Vancouver Canucks at some point over the first twenty seasons of the team. Kurtenbach was captain for the first four seasons of the Canucks' existence, from 1970-71 through 1973-74. Stan Smyl is the longest serving captain of the Canucks. He was given the honor in the eight seasons from 1982-83 to 1989-90. The other four individuals all served as captain at various times between Kurtenbach and Smyl.

SECOND PERIOD - BENCH BOSSES

1. Who were the three longest serving head coaches who were still in that capacity with their NHL teams at the end of the 2002-03 season?

Paul Maurice, Jacques Martin and Joel Quenneville. Paul Maurice began coaching the Hartford Whalers/Carolina Hurricanes in November of 1995 and has been head coach for 644 regular season games and 35 playoff games through the end of the 2002-03 season. Jacques Martin took the position with the Ottawa Senators in January of 1996. Martin has been head coach for 610 Ottawa Senator regular season games and 62 playoff games. Joel Quenneville assumed head coaching responsibilities with the St. Louis Blues in January of 1997. He has been behind the bench for 532 regular season and 68 playoff games with the Blues.

2. How many teams made head coaching changes during the 2002-03 NHL season?

Eight of the NHL's thirty teams made head coaching changes at some point during the 2002-03 season.

Coaching Changes during the 2002-03 NHL Season

Team	Date	Coaching Change
San Jose Sharks	Dec 1	Darryl Sutter replaced by interim coach Doug Wilson
	Dec 4	Ron Wilson appointed coach
Calgary Flames	Dec 3	Greg Gilbert replaced by interim coach Al MacNeil
	Dec 28	Darryl Sutter appointed coach
Colorado Avalanche	Dec 18	Bob Hartley replaced by Tony Granato
Atlanta Thrashers	Dec 26	Curt Fraser replaced by GM Don Waddell
	Jan 14	Bob Hartley appointed coach
Columbus Blue Jackets	Jan 7	Dave King replaced by GM Doug MacLean
Montreal Canadiens	Jan 17	Michel Therrien replaced by Claude Julien
New York Rangers	Jan 30	Bryan Trottier replaced by GM Glen Sather
Boston Bruins	Mar 19	Robbie Ftorek replaced by GM Mike O'Connell

3. Name the four NHL teams that Detroit's head coach Dave Lewis played on during his career.

Dave Lewis entered the NHL in 1973-74 with the New York Islanders. He played with the Islanders until just prior to their Stanley Cup victory in 1980, when he was traded to the Los Angeles Kings. Following three full seasons in Los Angeles, he was traded to the New Jersey Devils where he spent three more seasons. Lewis then signed as a free agent with the Detroit Red Wings in 1986. He saw his final action as a player in November of 1987, and then joined the Red Wings' coaching staff. He served as an assistant coach for a number of years, most recently under Scotty Bowman, until taking over the head coaching duties in July of 2002.

4. Name the three American-born individuals who have been head coach of a Stanley Cup-winning NHL team through 2003.

Leo Dandurand was born in Bourbonnais, Illinois. Dandurand led the 1923-24 Montreal Canadiens to a Cup victory. Bill Stewart, who was born in Fitchburg, Massachusetts, was behind the bench when the 1937-38 Chicago Black Hawks captured the Stanley Cup. The most recent American-born head coach to win the Stanley Cup was Bob Johnson with the 1990-91 Pittsburgh Penguins. Johnson was born in Farmington, Minnesota.

5. Name the only individual who played and coached for both the Montreal Canadiens and the Los Angeles Kings.

Bob Berry played his first two NHL games with the Montreal Canadiens in 1968-69. He was dealt to the Los Angeles Kings prior to the 1970-71 season. Berry played in the next seven seasons for the Kings. He became the bench boss of Los Angeles for the three seasons from 1978-79 to 1980-81. He also coached Montreal from 1981-82 until late in the 1983-84 season, when he was replaced by Jacques Lemaire. Berry has since served as head coach of both the Pittsburgh Penguins and the St. Louis Blues.

6. Name the four Toronto Maple Leaf coaches to lead the team to at least forty wins in a single season.

Coach	Year	Wins
Joe Primeau	1950-51	41
Roger Neilson	1977-78	41
Pat Burns	1992-93	44
	1993-94	43
Pat Quinn	1998-99	45
	1999-2000	45
	2001-02	43
	2002-03	44

7. Name the two NHL coaches who had a gap of fourteen years between their first and second appearance as a head coach in a Stanley Cup final.

Pat Quinn was the coach of the Philadelphia Flyers who lost the 1980 final to the New York Islanders. Quinn was again on the losing side fourteen years later when his Vancouver Canucks were defeated by the New York Rangers. Pat Burns was head coach of the Montreal Canadiens when they were defeated by the Calgary Flames in the 1989 Stanley Cup final. Burns had better luck the second time around when his 2003 New Jersey Devils captured the Stanley Cup over the Anaheim Mighty Ducks.

8. Name the brothers who both served as head coach of the Detroit Red Wings.

Johnny and Larry Wilson were both members of the Detroit Red Wings, among other teams, during their playing careers in the 1950s. Johnny went on to coach four different NHL franchises in seven seasons, including the Detroit Red Wings in 1971-72 and 1972-73. Larry's only head coaching experience in the NHL was a thirty-six game stint in 1976-77 with the Detroit Red Wings. Larry is the father of Ron Wilson who has served as head coach with Anaheim, Washington and San Jose.

9. Name the four individuals who held the head coaching position with the New Jersey Devils during a Stanley Cup-winning season.

Coach	New Jersey Cup-Winning Season
Jacques Lemaire	1994-95
Robbie Ftorek	1999-2000
Larry Robinson	1999-2000
Pat Burns	2002-03

10. Name the individual who was a head coach during Patrick Roy's first and final NHL game.

Jacques Lemaire was the head coach of the Montreal Canadiens when Patrick Roy played a single game in the 1984-85 season. Lemaire was behind the bench as head coach for the Minnesota Wild when they eliminated the Colorado Avalanche in game seven of the Western Conference quarter-final in 2003. This was Patrick Roy's final game.

11. Name the brothers who have been head coach of both the Florida Panthers and the Washington Capitals.

Bryan and Terry Murray have both been the head coach of the Washington Capitals and the Florida Panthers.

12. Name the two individuals who were selected as the coaches for the First and Second NHL All-Star Teams for the five years from 1930-31 through 1934-35.

Lester Patrick was selected as First All-Star Team coach for six consecutive seasons from 1930-31 through 1935-36. Dick Irvin Sr. of the Chicago Black Hawks took the honor of being the Second Team coach in 1930-31. He was selected again to the Second Team the following four seasons as coach of the Toronto Maple Leafs. The NHL abandoned naming All-Star coaches after the 1945-46 season.

13. Can you name the first four coaches of the St. Louis Blues? (Hint: They are members of the Hockey Hall of Fame.)

Lynn Patrick, Scotty Bowman, Al Arbour and Sid Abel all coached the team at various times between 1967-68 and 1972-73.

14. Who was the head coach for Team Canada in their gold medal wins at both the 1997 and 2003 men's World Championships?

Andy Murray, who has been head coach of the Los Angeles Kings since 1999, was head coach of the Canadian team for both of these World Championships.

15. How many individuals have won the Jack Adams Award as the NHL's top coach and also played for the Montreal Canadiens at some point in their career?

Five individuals have been presented with the Jack Adams Award and also skated as a Montreal Canadien.

Player/Coach	*Jack Adams Award*	*Montreal Seasons*
Red Berenson	1980-81 St. Louis Blues	1961-62 to 1965-66
Orval Tessier	1982-83 Chicago Black Hawks	1954-55
Glen Sather	1985-86 Edmonton Oilers	1974-75
Bob Murdoch	1989-90 Winnipeg Jets	1970-71 to 1972-73
Jacques Lemaire	1993-94 New Jersey Devils	1967-68 to 1978-79
	2002-03 Minnesota Wild	

16. Name the only coach to win the Jack Adams Award in consecutive seasons.

Jacques Demers of the Detroit Red Wings won the Jack Adams Award as top NHL coach in both 1986-87 and 1987-88.

17. Who was the first head coach of the Vancouver Canucks in the NHL?

Hal Laycoe coached the Canucks during their first two NHL seasons in 1970-71 and 1971-72.

18. Name the individual who coached the losing team in the NHL All-Star Game in four consecutive years.

Fred Shero was head coach for the losing Campbell Conference All-Stars in four consecutive games between 1975 and 1978. The closest he came to a win was in his final appearance as an All-Star coach in 1978, when the Wales defeated his Campbells 3-2 in overtime in a game held in Buffalo.

19. How did Roger Neilson do in his single appearance as a head coach in an NHL All-Star game?

Roger Neilson's Campbell Conference All-Stars soundly defeated the Wales Conference, coached by Al Arbour, by a score of 9-3 in the 1983 All-Star Game held in the Nassau County Coliseum. Neilson was selected as head coach based on the appearance of his Vancouver Canucks in the Stanley Cup final against Arbour's Islanders the previous spring.

20. How many times was Scotty Bowman a head coach at an NHL All-Star game?

Scotty Bowman was the head coach at an NHL All-Star game on thirteen occasions. Bowman had a record of seven wins, five losses and one tie during these games. His first appearance as an All-Star coach was in 1969 when he led the West to a 3-3 tie with the Eastern All-Stars. The opponent's coach was the legendary Toe Blake. Bowman most frequently faced Pat Quinn as the opposition's head coach. He did this on three occasions, including Scotty's final appearance as head coach for the 2002 All-Star Game. Bowman's World Team defeated the North American All-Stars 8-5 in this game.

THIRD PERIOD - ALL-STARS

1. Nicklas Lidstrom of the Detroit Red Wings was voted to the NHL First All-Star Team for six consecutive seasons from 1997-98 through 2002-03. Name the last player to be selected First All-Star in at least six consecutive seasons.

Wayne Gretzky was selected First All-Star at center for seven consecutive seasons from 1980-81 through 1986-87. Bobby Orr was the last defenseman to attain this, being First All-Star in eight consecutive seasons from 1967-68 through 1974-75. Ray Bourque came close to achieving this feat when he was selected a First All-Star in five consecutive seasons from 1989-90 through 1993-94.

2. Why did the NHL First All-Star Team of the 1937-38 season have eight individuals on it?

From 1930-31 through to the 1945-46 season, the NHL First All-Star Team included a coach. In 1937-38, there was also a tie for the right wing position between Cecil Dillon of the New York Rangers and Gordie Drillon of the Toronto Maple Leafs.

1937-38 NHL First All-Star Team

Position	Player	Team
Goal	Tiny Thompson	Boston Bruins
Defense	Eddie Shore	Boston Bruins
Defense	Babe Siebert	Montreal Canadiens
Center	Bill Cowley	Boston Bruins
Left Wing	Paul Thompson	Chicago Black Hawks
Right Wing (tie)	Cecil Dillon	New York Rangers
	Gordie Drillon	Toronto Maple Leafs
Coach	Lester Patrick	New York Rangers

3. How many times has an individual been selected to the NHL First All-Star Team for two consecutive seasons while playing for different teams?

This has happened on three different occasions. Doug Harvey, the most recent to do this, was a First Team All-Star on defense with the Montreal Canadiens in 1960-61 and was selected again the following year as a member of the New York Rangers. Goaltender Glenn Hall made the First All-Star Team with the Detroit Red Wings in 1956-57 and as a member of the Chicago Black Hawks in 1957-58. The first player to do this was Babe Siebert. He was a member of the Boston Bruins when he was selected First Team All-Star in 1935-36 and had the same honor the following season as a member of the Montreal Canadiens.

4. Name the brothers who combined for the most appearances in NHL All-Star games without ever playing in the same game.

Brothers Jean and Marcel Pronovost appeared in a combined total of fifteen NHL All-Star games while never playing in the same game. Marcel participated in eleven games, his first being in 1950 and his final NHL All-Star appearance in 1968, while Jean appeared in four consecutive All-Star games between 1975 and 1978.

5. Who was the first player to represent Colorado in an NHL All-Star game?

Wilf Paiement represented the Colorado Rockies in the 30th NHL All-Star Game held in Vancouver on Tuesday, January 25, 1977. Paiement was a member of the Campbell Conference All-Stars who lost 4-3 to the Wales

Conference in the annual classic. Peter Forsberg and Joe Sakic were the first representatives of the Colorado Avalanche at an NHL All-Star game, when it was held in Boston in 1996.

6. Charlie Gardiner of the Chicago Black Hawks was named First All-Star Team goalie in three of his last four seasons. Name the goaltender who prevented him from being selected to this position for all four seasons.

John Ross Roach of the Detroit Red Wings was selected as the First All-Star Team goalie for the 1932-33 season, with Charlie Gardiner as the Second Team goaltender. Gardiner had been selected as the First Team goalie in 1930-31, 1931-32 and was also selected for the First Team in 1933-34, his final season prior to his tragic death in June of 1934. Roach was playing in his twelfth NHL season, his first in Detroit, following a solid career in Toronto and with the Rangers in New York. This would be Roach's only selection to an NHL All-Star Team and his last full season in the league. He played parts of the next two seasons with the Red Wings before retiring in 1935.

7. When was the NHL All-Star game last held in the same city for two consecutive calendar years?

The last time the annual All-Star event was held in the same city for two consecutive years was in 1963 and 1964, when Toronto was the host. At that time, the game was held in October featuring the Stanley Cup winner playing a team of NHL All-Stars. While Montreal won consecutive Cups in 1965 and 1966, and would have hosted the All-Star game in two consecutive years, they didn't get the chance as no All-Star game was played in 1966. In 1966-67, the scheduling was changed and the game was moved from the fall to January of 1967. The game began to rotate from city to city in 1970.

8. Who scored the first hat trick in an NHL All-Star game?

Ted Lindsay of the Detroit Red Wings scored three goals on October 8, 1950, when the Red Wings defeated the NHL All-Stars 7-1.

9. Name the only year in which the six members of the NHL First All-Star Team came from a single conference since realignment in 1993-94.

The 2001-02 NHL First All-Star Team was composed entirely of players from the Western Conference.

2001-02 NHL First All-Star Team

Postion	Player	Team
Goal	Patrick Roy	Colorado Avalanche
Defense	Nicklas Lidstrom	Detroit Red Wings
Defense	Chris Chelios	Detroit Red Wings
Centre	Joe Sakic	Colorado Avalanche
Left Wing	Markus Nasland	Vancouver Canucks
Right Wing	Jarome Iginla	Calgary Flames

10. Name the two NHL officials who have skated in ten NHL All-Star games.

Neil Armstrong and Matt Pavelich had lengthy NHL careers as linesmen and were each selected to officiate in the league's All-Star game on ten occasions. Pavelich began his career as an NHL linesman in 1956-57, although he didn't see any All-Star action until he was selected for the 1962 All-Star Game in Toronto. Pavelich's tenth All-Star game was the 1977 match in Vancouver. He was actually on the ice with the All-Stars for an eleventh time, when he was selected to do the lines in game two of the 1979 Challenge Cup. Armstrong started as a linesman in 1957-58 and was selected to work his first All-Star game in 1960 in Montreal. Armstrong went on to officiate in the NHL for twenty seasons. His last All-Star appearance was the 1976 match in Philadelphia. During their careers, Armstrong and Pavelich teamed up for five of their All-Star games in the 1960s. Both officials were inducted into the Hockey Hall of Fame to recognize their outstanding careers: Pavelich in 1987 and Neil Armstrong in 1991.

11. When was the last time there was a scoreless twenty-minute period of hockey in an NHL All-Star game?

The 1986 All-Star Game, which was held in Hartford, had a scoreless first period. The Wales Conference defeated the Campbells 4-3 in overtime.

12. What was the first year that no Toronto Maple Leaf participated in the NHL All-Star game?

The 2003 NHL All-Star Game was the first time that a Maple Leaf did not take part. Both Mats Sundin and Ed Belfour were slated to play in the game, but were unable to participate due to injury.

13. Name the two individuals who represented the Ottawa Senators in the 1993 All-Star Game.

Peter Sidorkiewicz and Brad Marsh represented the Ottawa Senators on the Wales Conference All-Stars in the 1993 All-Star Game held at the Montreal Forum. Marsh recorded a goal and an assist, while Sidorkiewicz played goal in the second period letting in two goals on sixteen shots. This was the only NHL All-Star game appearance for both players as they helped the Wales Conference trounce the Campbell Conference 16-6 in the 44th NHL All-Star Game.

14. Name the six individuals who were selected by fan ballot to be members of the NHL All-Stars in the Rendez-Vous '87 series versus the Soviet Union.

NHL All-Stars for Rendez-Vous '87 - Fan Ballot Selections

Position	Player	Team
Goalie	Clint Malarchuk	Quebec Nordiques
Defense	Paul Coffey	Edmonton Oilers
Defense	Mark Howe	Philadelphia Flyers
Forward	Mario Lemieux	Pittsburgh Penguins
Forward	Michel Goulet	Quebec Nordiques
Forward	Mike Bossy	New York Islanders

15. Name the last player to be named MVP of an NHL All-Star game played at his home rink.

Ray Bourque was named MVP of the 46th NHL All-Star Game, held at the FleetCenter in Boston on Saturday, January 20, 1996. Bourque scored the winning goal for the Eastern Conference All-Stars with thirty-eight seconds remaining in the game. His shot beat goaltender Felix Potvin to give the Eastern Conference a 5-4 victory over the Western Conference.

16. Name the first player who was selected to the NHL First All-Star Team as a member of the Vancouver Canucks.

The Canucks were in their twenty-fourth NHL season before a Vancouver player was selected to the First All-Star Team. Pavel Bure was chosen as the First All-Star right winger for the 1993-94 season.

17. Name the three members of the 1973-74 Stanley Cup-winning Philadelphia Flyers who were selected to the year-end All-Star Teams.

Goaltender Bernie Parent was selected as a member of the NHL First All-Star Team, while centre Bobby Clarke and defenseman Barry Ashbee were both members of the NHL Second All-Star Team for 1973-74. Ashbee played his last NHL hockey that season, when he suffered a career-ending eye injury during the semi-final in which Philadelphia defeated the New York Rangers.

18. Name the only three individuals selected as left winger to the NHL First All-Star Team in the fourteen seasons between 1959-60 and 1972-73.

Bobby Hull was selected as the NHL First All-Star Team left winger in ten of these seasons, while Frank Mahovlich was chosen in three: 1960-61, 1962-63 and 1972-73. Johnny Bucyk was named the left winger on the NHL First All-Star Team in 1970-71.

19. When was the last time that one NHL team had four players selected to the First All-Star Team?

The 1976-77 NHL All-Star Team included four members of the Montreal Canadiens: goaltender Ken Dryden, defenseman Larry Robinson, right winger Guy Lafleur and left winger Steve Shutt. Defenseman Borje Salming of the Toronto Maple Leafs and center Marcel Dionne of the Los Angeles Kings rounded out the First All-Star Team for that season.

20. Name the last goalie to have played in all three periods of an NHL All-Star game.

Pete Peeters of the Philadelphia Flyers played in all three periods of the 1980 All-Star Game as a member of the Campbell Conference All-Stars. Starting Campbell goalie, Tony Esposito, injured his hand just after the fifteen-minute mark of the first period. He was replaced by Peeters who played the remaining forty-five minutes of the game. The Campbells were defeated by the Wales Conference 6-3. Before this game, the last time a goaltender had played in all three periods of an All-Star game was in 1965, when three goaltenders did so. Glenn Hall played the entire game for the NHL All-Stars, while Gump Worsley and Charlie Hodge of the Montreal Canadiens were rotated throughout the entire game, approximately every five minutes, by coach Toe Blake.

Bobby Clarke led the 1974 Philadelphia Flyers to a Stanley Cup victory over Bobby Orr and Gilles Gilbert of the Boston Bruins.

PHOTO REPLAY

1. Who was the captain of the Philadelphia Flyers prior to Bobby Clarke?

Ed Van Impe was named the Flyers' captain for the 1968-69 season and remained in that role until Bobby Clarke replaced him as team captain in January of 1973. Clarke, who was twenty-three, became the youngest captain in NHL history at the time.

2. Name the only year in which Bobby Orr and Bobby Clarke were both named to the NHL First All-Star Team.

Both players were selected as members of the First All-Star Team for the 1974-75 season. This was Orr's last of eight consecutive selections to the NHL First All-Star Team, while it was Clarke's first of two consecutive selections.

3. Which of these two players was the highest scorer in the 1974 Stanley Cup final?

Bobby Clarke and Bobby Orr's only meeting in a Stanley Cup final took place in 1974. While Clarke's Flyers captured the Cup in six games, it was Orr who was the leading scorer in the series. Orr recorded three goals and four assists for seven points, while Clarke was the leading scorer for the Flyers with three goals and three assists for six points in the six games.

4. Name the only player, other than Bobby Orr and Bobby Clarke, to win the Hart Trophy in the seven seasons between 1969-70 and 1975-76.

Phil Esposito won the Hart Trophy as the NHL's most valuable player in the 1973-74 season. Orr was presented with the Hart Trophy for three straight seasons between 1969-70 and 1971-72, while Clarke was awarded the trophy in 1972-73 and again in the two seasons following Esposito's Hart Trophy win.

Puckstoppers

The appeal of being a goaltender who faces blistering shots and phenomenal pressure is something that many fans of the game find hard to understand. Yet for those who put on the pads and face mask, the adrenaline rush experienced in net is seldom equaled anywhere else. From pioneers like Vezina to Original Six heroes like Bower and Plante, the goalie was always evolving and responding to the changing game. Styles shifted from stand-up to butterfly and icons like Fuhr and Roy amazed fans with their unbelievable abilities. A new generation of goalies, such as Brodeur and Giguere, has now emerged and continues the quest to provide the ultimate defense.

FIRST PERIOD - WHO AM I?

1. I am the only NHL goalie to have recorded four shutouts in a playoff year, but not reach the Stanley Cup final.

Patrick Lalime recorded four shutouts as a member of the Ottawa Senators in the 2002 playoff year. Lalime earned three shutouts in the opening series against the Philadelphia Flyers and started the Eastern Conference semi-final with a 5-0 shutout over the Toronto Maple Leafs. However, the Leafs eliminated the Senators in seven games.

2. I hold the record for the most wins by a goaltender in a single NHL season.

Bernie Parent recorded forty-seven wins as a member of the Philadelphia Flyers in the 1973-74 season.

3. I was Bernie Parent's backup in the Flyers' first Cup-winning season of 1973-74.

Bobby Taylor was the only other goaltender to see action with the Philadelphia Flyers in 1973-74. Taylor played in a total of eight games, with a record of 3-3-0 and a goals-against average of 4.26. Taylor was in net for three games in the following Cup season of 1974-75 with the Flyers, but his backup role to Bernie Parent had been taken by Wayne Stephenson. The Flyers had picked up Stephenson in a trade with the St. Louis Blues in September of 1974.

4. I played goal for both the Quebec Nordiques and the Edmonton Oilers in 1979-80.

Ron Low was claimed by Quebec from the Detroit Red Wings in the NHL Expansion Draft in June of 1979. Low played a total of fifteen games with the Nordiques and also saw action with the Syracuse Firebirds of the American Hockey League, before he was picked up by Edmonton in a trade in March of 1980. Low had a record of 8-2-1 in the eleven games he played for the Oilers to finish out the 1979-80 season. He also played in three playoff games with the Oilers that year. Low played for the Oilers until 1983 when he was traded to the New Jersey Devils. Earlier in his career, he also played net for Toronto, Washington and Detroit. After his NHL playing career ended in 1985, he served as a head coach in the NHL with both the Edmonton Oilers and the New York Rangers.

5. I was a goalie on the losing team in the first two NHL playoff games which ended in the fifth overtime period.

Ron Tugnutt was in net for the Pittsburgh Penguins when they were defeated by the Philadelphia Flyers 2-1 on Keith Primeau's goal at 12:01 of the fifth overtime period on May 4, 2000. Nearly three years later, Tugnutt was on the bench as the backup goalie to Marty Turco when Petr Sykora scored to give the Anaheim Mighty Ducks a 4-3 win in the fifth overtime of game one of the Western Conference semi-final on April 24, 2003.

6. I am the only goaltender to win the Calder Trophy and not see a minute of NHL action the following season.

Lorne "Gump" Worsley won the Calder in 1952-53 as a member of the New York Rangers. However, the following season when he asked for a small raise in salary, he was shipped off to the minors and replaced by Johnny Bower.

7. I played goal with four different clubs in over 600 NHL regular season and playoff games through the end of the 2002-03 season and yet I have never been traded.

Goaltender Arturs Irbe was selected 196th overall by the Minnesota North Stars in the 1989 Entry Draft. Irbe never played with the Minnesota North Stars, as he continued to tend net for Dynamo Riga in the Soviet League through 1991. He was claimed by the San Jose Sharks from the North Stars in the Dispersal Draft in 1991. Irbe played the next five seasons with the Sharks. In 1996, he signed as a free agent with the Dallas Stars for one season, and then went to Vancouver as a free agent in 1997. Following a season with Vancouver, he joined the Carolina Hurricanes through free agency, where he was still playing in 2002-03.

8. I was selected to the WHA First All-Star Team in the same season that my brother was selected to the NHL First All-Star Team.

Dave Dryden of the Edmonton Oilers was selected as the goaltender on the First All-Star Team in the final season of the WHA, 1978-79. His brother Ken was selected as the goaltender of the First NHL All-Star Team that same season, which was Ken's final season playing goal.

9. I played goal in a record nine consecutive All-Star games.

Glenn Hall tended goal in nine consecutive All-Star games between 1960 and 1969. In 1961, he played for the Stanley Cup champion Black Hawks as they faced the NHL All-Stars. In the other eight games, he was selected as an All-Star goaltender. Hall also holds the record for the most appearances in an All-Star game as a goaltender. He played in thirteen of the fourteen games held between 1955 and 1969, only missing the game in 1959.

10. I was selected by the fans as a goaltender for the NHL All-Stars in the 1979 Challenge Cup.

Tony Esposito of the Chicago Black Hawks was selected by fan voting as a goaltender for the NHL All-Stars in the 1979 Challenge Cup against the Soviet Union. Gerry Cheevers and Ken Dryden were the other two goaltenders, selected by the NHL management team, who rounded out the roster. Dryden played the first two matches while Cheevers was in net for the final game. Tony Esposito was the only one of the three goalies not to play in the 1979 Challenge Cup.

11. I played the most minutes of any goaltender in the 2002-03 NHL season.

Marc Denis of the Columbus Blue Jackets played 4511 minutes in goal in 2002-03. Denis appeared in 77 of the Blue Jackets' 82 games during the season. Denis' goaltending time set an NHL record for a season.

12. I began and ended my career with the New York Rangers, but won a Cup as Patrick Roy's backup with Montreal in 1986.

Doug Soetaert played in six NHL seasons with the New York Rangers before being traded to the Winnipeg Jets in 1981. After three seasons in Winnipeg, he was dealt to the Montreal Canadiens where he played for two seasons, including 1985-86, where he was backup to Patrick Roy in Montreal's Cup-winning year. Soetaert left the Canadiens following the Cup victory, signing as a free agent with the Rangers for one final season in 1986-87.

13. I arrived in Buffalo in February of 1975 and took the Sabres all the way to the Stanley Cup final.

Gerry Desjardins had played goal with the Los Angeles Kings, the Chicago Black Hawks and the New York Islanders when he left the NHL for the WHA in 1974. He played in forty-one games as a member of the Michigan/Baltimore Stags in 1974-75. Desjardins returned to the NHL with Buffalo in February of 1975, as the Sabres obtained his rights from the New York Islanders. He took over as the starting goaltender from Gary Bromley, who was being backed up by Roger Crozier. Desjardins played in fifteen playoff games and Crozier saw action in five, as the Sabres eliminated Chicago in the quarter-final and Montreal in the semi-final before being defeated in a six-game final series by the Philadelphia Flyers.

14. I am the only goaltender who won forty games in four separate NHL seasons.

Martin Brodeur of the New Jersey Devils reached the forty-win mark for a fourth season with forty-one victories in 2002-03. Brodeur had previously won forty-three games in 1997-98 and 1999-2000 and forty-two games in 2000-01.

15. I played goal in 464 regular season NHL games before I saw my first playoff action.

Gilles Meloche was a solid number one goaltender with some of the NHL's weaker teams in the 1970s. Meloche was traded by the Chicago Black Hawks to the California Golden Seals in October of 1971. Meloche played in an average of fifty games in each of his five seasons with the Golden Seals. They relocated to Cleveland as the Barons for the two seasons of 1976-77 and 1977-78, where Meloche remained the first goaltender. Meloche then moved on to Minnesota when the North Stars purchased the players of the Cleveland Barons franchise. He saw action in Minnesota for two seasons before finally playing in his first NHL playoff game in 1980. Meloche was in the playoffs for six consecutive years with the North Stars. His final three seasons were with the Pittsburgh Penguins. Meloche retired after the 1987-88 season.

16. I had the best save percentage among regular goaltenders in the 2002-03 NHL season.

Marty Turco of the Dallas Stars recorded a save percentage of .932 in the fifty-five games he played with the Dallas Stars in 2002-03. Turco let in only ninety-two goals on 1359 shots during the season.

17. I was Billy Smith's goaltending partner for three of the four years when the Islanders won the Stanley Cup.

Rollie Melanson joined the New York Islanders in 1980-81 for the Islanders' second Stanley Cup, after Glenn "Chico" Resch had been traded to the Colorado Rockies. Melanson played in thirty-six regular season and three playoff games with the Islanders in 1981-82. He then played in forty-four games compared to Billy Smith's forty-one in the 1982-83 season. Melanson was selected as the Second All-Star Team goalie in 1982-83 and shared the William M. Jennings Trophy with Billy Smith. Melanson saw only eighty-seven minutes of playoff action in six games compared to Billy Smith's 962 minutes in seventeen games in 1983. Melanson was traded in 1984 and moved on to play with the Minnesota North Stars, the Los Angeles Kings, the New Jersey Devils and the Montreal Canadiens. His NHL career ended in 1991-92.

18. I recorded a shutout in the deciding game of the 1979 Challenge Cup.

Vladimir Myshkin replaced Vladislav Tretiak for the third and deciding game of the 1979 Challenge Cup. The Soviet Union defeated the NHL All-Stars 6-0 in this game held on February 11, 1979.

19. I recorded the most losses by a goaltender in a single NHL season.

Gary Smith of the California Golden Seals recorded forty-eight losses in seventy-one games played as a member of the California Golden Seals in 1970-71.

20. I am the only goaltender with a surname beginning with "Z" to have played in the NHL between 1917-18 and 2002-03.

Mike Zanier played net in three games for the Edmonton Oilers in the 1984-85 season. Zanier, a native of Trail, British Columbia, saw action with several teams in the Western Hockey League in the early 1980s and was signed as a free agent by the Oilers in October of 1983. He played in the AHL with Moncton and Nova Scotia before his brief goaltending stint with Edmonton. After a season with Indianapolis in the IHL, he moved on to Europe, where he played predominantly in the Italian leagues through the 1990s. He has also played for Italy in international competitions, including the 1992 Olympics.

SECOND PERIOD - MULTIPLE CHOICE

1. Which NHL team recorded the most shutouts during the 2002-03 regular season?

a) Anaheim   b) Dallas   c) New Jersey   d) Ottawa

b) The Dallas Stars shutout their opponents on eleven occasions during 2002-03. Marty Turco was in the Dallas net for seven shutouts, while Ron Tugnutt had four.

2. What is the greatest number of seasons that a goaltender has played in the National Hockey League?

a) 18   b) 19   c) 20   d) 21

d) 21. Both Terry Sawchuk and Lorne "Gump" Worsley saw action in a total of twenty-one NHL seasons. Sawchuk played in every season between 1949-50 and 1969-70, spending the majority of that time in Detroit, but also seeing stints with Boston, Toronto, Los Angeles and the New York Rangers. Worsley only missed one season between 1952-53 and 1973-74, in a career with the New York Rangers, the Montreal Canadiens and the Minnesota North Stars.

3. How many goalies have won the Vezina Trophy in at least four consecutive seasons?

a) 1   b) 2   c) 3   d) 4

c) 3. All three goalies who have achieved this have done so as members of the Montreal Canadiens. Bill Durnan racked up four consecutive Vezina wins between 1943-44 and 1946-47. Jacques Plante had an unprecedented five consecutive Vezina-winning seasons, from 1955-56 through 1959-60. Ken Dryden had the honor of winning the trophy four consecutive times between 1975-76 through 1978-79.

4. How many goalies recorded shutouts for the St. Louis Blues during the 2002-03 season?

a) 4   b) 5   c) 6   d) 7

b) 5. Five of the seven goalies who tended net for St. Louis during 2002-03 recorded shutouts. Brent Johnson, Fred Brathwaite and Chris Osgood each had two shutouts, while Curtis Sanford and Tom Barrasso both recorded singles.

5. How many times has the Hart Trophy been awarded to a goaltender who was not placed on the season-ending NHL First All-Star Team?

a) 1   b) 2   c) 3   d) 4

d) 4. On four of the seven occasions that a goaltender has been awarded a Hart Trophy, the winning goalie has not been named First All-Star. Most recently, Jose Theodore won the Hart Trophy in 2002, but was placed on the Second All-Star Team. Charlie Rayner of the New York Rangers won the Hart in 1949-50, but was also placed on the Second All-Star Team. Roy Worters of the New York Americans won the award in 1928-29, which was two seasons prior to the first time an All-Star Team was named at the end of the season. Al Rollins of the Chicago Black Hawks also won the award in 1953-54, but was not elected to either All-Star Team. The other three times a goaltender won the Hart Trophy, they were placed on the First All-Star Team. Jacques Plante of the Montreal Canadiens had the honor in 1961-62 and Dominik Hasek was awarded the Hart in two consecutive seasons, 1996-97 and 1997-98.

6. How many goaltenders have been selected as a member of either the First or Second NHL All-Star Team as a Washington Capital?

a) 1   b) 2   c) 3   d) 4

c) 3. Pat Riggin was the first Washington Capitals' goaltender to be named to an All-Star Team. He was selected as the Second All-Star goalie in 1983-84. The two Washington goalies who have been selected to the First All-Star Team are Jim Carey in 1995-96 and Olaf Kolzig in 1999-2000.

7. How many goalies have played for both the Calgary Flames and the Edmonton Oilers?

a) 1   b) 2   c) 3   d) 4

b) 2. Fred Brathwaite and Grant Fuhr are the only two goaltenders who have played for both the Calgary Flames and the Edmonton Oilers. Brathwaite and Fuhr began their careers with the Oilers and ended up teammates for one season with the Flames. Fuhr, a member of the Hall of Fame, saw action in ten seasons with the Edmonton Oilers from 1981-82 through 1990-91. He finished his career in 1999-2000 as a member of the Calgary Flames. Fred Brathwaite played in three seasons with the Edmonton Oilers from 1993-94 through 1995-96, and saw another three seasons with the Calgary Flames from 1998-99 through 2000-01.

8. How many of the first thirty-eight winners of the Vezina Trophy have not gone on to be named members of the Hockey Hall of Fame?

a) 6   b) 8   c) 10   d) 12

a) 6. Of the thirty-eight times that the Vezina Trophy was awarded from 1927 to 1964, there were only six winners who did not go on to be named members of the Hockey Hall of Fame.

Vezina-Winning Season	Goaltender	Team
1934-35	Lorne Chabot	Chicago Black Hawks
1936-37	Normie Smith	Detroit Red Wings
1939-40	Dave Kerr	New York Rangers
1942-43	Johnny Mowers	Detroit Red Wings
1950-51	Al Rollins	Toronto Maple Leafs
1963-64	Charlie Hodge	Montreal Canadiens

9. Name the last goalie to play in the NHL who had seen game action in the Original Six era.

a) Roger Crozier   b) Cesare Maniago
c) Gary Smith   d) Rogie Vachon

d) Rogie Vachon played with the 1966-67 Montreal Canadiens and saw his final NHL action in the 1981-82 season with the Boston Bruins.

10. How many goaltenders who played during the 2002-03 NHL season were previous winners of the Vezina Trophy?

a) 4   b) 5   c) 6   d) 7

b) 5.

Goaltender	2002-03 Team	Vezina Trophy-Winning Season
Jose Theodore	Montreal Canadiens	Montreal, 2001-02
Olaf Kolzig	Washington Capitals	Washington, 1999-2000
Ed Belfour	Toronto Maple Leafs	Chicago, 1990-91, 1992-93
Patrick Roy	Colorado Avalanche	Montreal, 1988-89, 1989-90, 1991-92
Tom Barrasso	St. Louis Blues	Buffalo, 1983-84

11. Which goalie was not selected by the New Jersey Devils in the 1990 Entry Draft?

a) Martin Brodeur   b) Mike Dunham
c) Corey Schwab   d) Chris Terreri

d) Chris Terreri. All of these goaltenders were drafted by the New Jersey Devils and have seen action with the club at various points in their careers. Terreri is the only one that was not selected in the 1990 NHL Entry Draft. Terreri was selected 87th overall in the 1983 Entry Draft by the New Jersey Devils. Brodeur, Dunham and Schwab were chosen 20th, 53rd and 200th overall in 1990.

12. Which team originally selected Jean-Sebastian Giguere in the NHL Entry Draft?

a) Anaheim Mighty Ducks   b) Calgary Flames
c) Carolina Hurricanes   d) Hartford Whalers

d) Hartford Whalers. Jean-Sebastian Giguere was selected 13th overall in the 1995 Entry Draft by the Hartford Whalers. Giguere played in eight games with Hartford in 1996-97. He was later traded to Calgary, after the Whalers relocated to Carolina as the Hurricanes. Calgary then traded Giguere to Anaheim for a draft choice in June of 2000.

13. How many future Hall of Fame goaltenders were traded by Detroit's general manager Jack Adams during the 1950s?

a) 1   b) 2   c) 3   d) 4

c) 3. Harry Lumley was dealt to Chicago following Detroit's Stanley Cup championship in 1950 to make room for Terry Sawchuk. Terry Sawchuk was traded to Boston in 1955 following Detroit's Cup victory and the goaltending job was given to Glenn Hall. Hall was then dealt to Chicago in 1957 and replaced by the returning Sawchuk.

14. How many goaltenders have been selected to the NHL First All-Star Team as a member of the Toronto Maple Leafs?

a) 2   b) 3   c) 4   d) 5

b) 3. Only Turk Broda, Harry Lumley and Johnny Bower have been selected as NHL First Team All-Stars while playing goal for the Maple Leafs. Broda was selected on two occasions, in 1940-41 and again in 1947-48; Lumley made the team in the two consecutive seasons of 1953-54 and 1954-55; and Bower's lone appearance on the NHL First All-Star Team was in 1960-61.

15. How many teams had only one goalie play for them in the 2003 playoffs?

a) 5   **b) 7**   **c) 9**   **d) 11**

b) Seven of the sixteen teams had only one goalie play for them for the entire 2003 playoffs.

Team	Goalie	GP
Ottawa Senators	Patrick Lalime	18
Dallas Stars	Marty Turco	12
Colorado Avalanche	Patrick Roy	7
St. Louis Blues	Chris Osgood	7
Toronto Maple Leafs	Ed Belfour	7
Washington Capitals	Olaf Kolzig	6
Detroit Red Wings	Curtis Joseph	4

16. How many goaltenders have been awarded the Bill Masterton Memorial Trophy?

a) 0   **b) 1**   **c) 2**   **d) 3**

d) 3. Glenn Resch, Mark Fitzpatrick and Jamie McLennan have all been awarded the Bill Masterton Trophy. The trophy is awarded annually to the player who best exemplifies the qualities of perseverance, sportsmanship and dedication to hockey. Glenn "Chico" Resch of the Colorado Rockies was the first goaltender awarded the Bill Masterton Trophy in 1982. Mark Fitzpatrick was a member of the New York Islanders when he received the trophy in 1992 and St. Louis Blue Jamie McLennan won the honor in 1998.

17. Which two New York Islander goalies hold the team record for the most wins in a single season?

a) Rollie Melanson   **b) Chris Osgood**
c) Glenn Resch   **d) Billy Smith**

b) and d) Both Billy Smith and Chris Osgood have won thirty-two games in a single season with the New York Islanders. Billy Smith accomplished this in the 1981-82 season. His record was duplicated by Chris Osgood in 2001-02.

18. How many goaltenders have won the Vezina Trophy as a member of the Philadelphia Flyers?

a) 1   b) 2   c) 3   d) 4

c) 3. Bernie Parent, Pelle Lindbergh and Ron Hextall. Parent was the first to achieve this, winning a Vezina in 1973-74 when he tied with Tony Esposito of the Chicago Black Hawks. He duplicated the achievement in 1974-75. Pelle Lindbergh received the Vezina in 1984-85. He was tragically killed in an automobile accident in November of 1985. Ron Hextall, the third Flyer to win the Vezina, received the honor in his rookie season of 1986-87.

19. How many goaltenders recorded a shutout for more than one team in the 2002-03 NHL season?

a) 0   b) 1   c) 2   d) 3

c) 2. Chris Osgood recorded shutouts for both the New York Islanders and the St. Louis Blues in 2002-03, while John Grahame registered shutouts with both the Boston Bruins and the Tampa Bay Lightning.

20. Who was second to Patrick Roy in NHL playoff appearances in goal at the end of the 2003 final?

a) Ed Belfour   b) Martin Brodeur
c) Grant Fuhr   d) Mike Vernon

c) Grant Fuhr, who played goal in 150 playoff games, is second to Patrick Roy in post-season appearances. Through the end of the 2003 playoffs, Ed Belfour had appeared in 148 and Martin Brodeur had played in 139 post-season games. Mike Vernon was in the net for 138 Stanley Cup playoff games. Patrick Roy was well ahead of all of them, having played in 247 playoff games at the time of his retirement following his 2003 Stanley Cup appearances.

THIRD PERIOD - EXPERT TRIVIA

1. Name the only three Hall of Fame members to have played goal for the Los Angeles Kings.

Hall of Fame Goalies	Season
Terry Sawchuk	1967-68
Billy Smith	1971-72
Grant Fuhr	1994-95

2. Name the two goalies who both recorded their first NHL shutout while facing each other in the 2002-03 season.

Michael Leighton of the Chicago Blackhawks and Zac Bierk of the Phoenix Coyotes both recorded their first NHL shutout when they faced each other on January 8, 2003.

3. Name the three goaltenders who have recorded the most shutouts in a single NHL playoff year.

Goalie	Team	GP	Shutouts	Playoff Year
Martin Brodeur	New Jersey	24	7	2003
Dominik Hasek	Detroit	23	6	2002
Jean-Sebastian Giguere	Anaheim	21	5	2003

Goalies have recorded four shutouts in a single playoff year on fourteen occasions between 1926 and 2002.

4. Name the Hall of Famer who was in goal for the last Stanley Cup victory of both the old Ottawa Senators franchise in 1927 and the Montreal Maroons in 1935.

Alex Connell began his NHL career in Ottawa and backstopped the Senators to the Cup in his third season in 1926-27. He led the Montreal Maroons to their final Stanley Cup victory in his second-last season in 1934-35. Connell saw action in a total of twelve NHL seasons, finishing his career with the Maroons.

5. Name the three former NHL goaltenders who were acting as general managers of an NHL team at the close of the 2002-03 season.

Ken Holland, Jim Rutherford and Wayne Thomas. Ken Holland had a brief career as an NHL goalie appearing in a total of four games in the 1980s with Hartford and Detroit. He has had a longer stay in the NHL as a general manager, serving in that capacity with the Detroit Red Wings since 1997-98. Jim Rutherford saw NHL action over thirteen seasons, largely with the Detroit Red Wings, but also with Pittsburgh, Toronto and Los Angeles. Rutherford has been general manager of the Hartford Whalers/Carolina Hurricanes since 1994. Wayne Thomas tended net for Montreal, Toronto and the Rangers in nine different NHL seasons.

Thomas became interim general manager for the San Jose Sharks, when Dean Lombardi was released from the position in March of 2003. Doug Wilson has since been appointed as San Jose's general manager for the 2003-04 NHL season.

6. Name the backup goaltenders to Martin Brodeur during the three Stanley Cup-winning seasons of the New Jersey Devils.

Chris Terreri was backup to Martin Brodeur in both 1994-95 and 1999-2000, while Corey Schwab was the Devils' second goaltender in 2002-03.

7. Name the first three individuals selected to the Hockey Hall of Fame who played their last NHL game in goal for Detroit.

Harry "Hap" Holmes, Cecil "Tiny" Thompson and Ed Giacomin. Hap Holmes played his early professional years with Toronto in both the NHA and the NHL. He then went on to play professional hockey in the west with both Seattle and Victoria, before returning to Detroit when they entered the NHL in 1926. Holmes played two seasons with the Detroit Cougars, before retiring in 1928. Holmes was inducted into the Hockey Hall of Fame in 1972. Tiny Thompson was traded to the Detroit Red Wings from the Boston Bruins in 1938-39, the eleventh of his twelve seasons in the league. Thompson was selected to the Hall of Fame in 1959. Ed Giacomin was in his eleventh NHL season when he was traded by the New York Rangers to the Detroit Red Wings in 1975. Giacomin wrapped up his thirteen year career in 1977-78 in Detroit. Giacomin was inducted into the Hockey Hall of Fame in 1987.

8. Name the four goalies who have been awarded the Conn Smythe Trophy as a member of the losing team in a Stanley Cup final.

Goalie	Finalist	Year
Roger Crozier	Detroit Red Wings	1966
Glenn Hall	St. Louis Blues	1968
Ron Hextall	Philadelphia Flyers	1987
Jean-Sebastien Giguere	Anaheim Mighty Ducks	2003

9. Name the first goaltender to have won the Vezina Trophy four times.

Cecil "Tiny" Thompson was the first goaltender to be awarded the Vezina Trophy on four occasions. Thompson had no back-to-back Vezina wins. He was first presented with the trophy in 1929-30 and his final Vezina honor was in 1937-38.

10. Name the four goalies who recorded the most shutouts in the 2002-03 NHL regular season.

Goalie	Team	Shutouts
Martin Brodeur	New Jersey Devils	9
Jean-Sebastien Giguere	Anaheim Mighty Ducks	8
Patrick Lalime	Ottawa Senators	8
Jocelyn Thibault	Chicago Blackhawks	8

11. Name the first four goalies who were winners of the Vezina Trophy, but did not take part in a playoff game in their winning season.

Roy Worters of the 1930-31 New York Americans was the only goaltender to have been awarded the Vezina Trophy on a team that did not see playoff action. Worters played all forty-four games for the Americans in 1930-31 and recorded an amazing 1.61 goals-against average and eight shutouts, but the Americans finished in fourth place in the Canadian Division and did not qualify for the playoffs. The other three Vezina winners that did not see playoff action during the season in which they won the award were: Charlie Hodge, Michel Larocque and Denis Herron. All three were backup goaltenders for the Montreal Canadiens. Charlie Hodge shared the Vezina with Lorne "Gump" Worsley, who was the Habs' only playoff netminder in 1965-66. Michel "Bunny" Larocque backed up Ken Dryden, but did not see any playoff action in their Vezina-winning seasons of 1976-77 and 1977-78. Richard Sevigny was the playoff goalie for the Canadiens while Denis Herron watched, in their Vezina Trophy-winning season of 1980-81.

12. Name the first four goalies to have their names on both the Vezina Trophy and William M. Jennings Trophy.

Denis Herron, Billy Smith, Bob Sauve and Tom Barrasso were the first four goalies to be awarded both the William M. Jennings and Vezina Trophies. The William M. Jennings Trophy was first awarded for the 1981-82 season to recognize any goaltenders playing in at least twenty-five games with the team with the best goals-against average. The lowest team goals-against average had been the criteria for the Vezina Trophy up until this point. However, beginning in 1981-82, the Vezina was awarded to the goalie selected as the outstanding goaltender of that season by the NHL general managers. Denis Herron was a co-winner of the Vezina with Richard Sevigny and Michel Larocque in 1980-81. He was also awarded the Jennings jointly with Rick Wamsley of the Montreal Canadiens in 1981-82. Billy Smith received the Vezina Trophy in 1981-82 and shared the Jennings with Rollie Melanson, his Islander teammate, the following year. Bob Sauve of the Buffalo Sabres won the Vezina with Don Edwards in 1979-80 and then shared the Jennings with Tom Barrasso in 1984-85. Tom Barrasso was the fourth individual to receive both trophies as he won the Vezina Trophy in 1983-84 with the Buffalo Sabres.

13. Name the only three individuals to have recorded at least fifteen shutouts as an NHL goalie in playoff competition as of 2003.

NHL Playoff Shutout Leaders after the 2003 Final

Shutouts	Goaltender	Teams
23	Patrick Roy	Montreal Canadiens, Colorado Avalanche
20	Martin Brodeur	New Jersey Devils
15	Curtis Joseph	St. Louis Blues, Edmonton Oilers, Toronto Maple Leafs

14. When was the last time that opposing goalies both recorded a point in a Stanley Cup final?

Martin Brodeur of the New Jersey Devils and Jean-Sebastian Giguere of the Anaheim Mighty Ducks both received assists in the 2003 Stanley Cup final. Brodeur assisted on Jeff Friesen's empty net goal at 19:38 of the third period in the first game, while Giguere assisted on Sandis Ozolinsh's goal at 14:47 of the second period in game three.

15. Name the only two goaltenders to have recorded five shutouts in a single WHA season.

Gerry Cheevers and Joe Daley. Cheevers recorded five shutouts with the Cleveland Crusaders in 1972-73, the first season of the WHA. Joe Daley also earned five shutouts in a WHA season, as a Winnipeg Jet in 1975-76.

16. Name the two veteran NHL goaltenders who played in the Olympics in three different decades.

Dominik Hasek and Mike Richter both saw action in the 1988, 1998 and 2002 Olympic Winter Games. Hasek represented Czechoslovakia in 1988 and the Czech Republic in 1998 and 2002. Richter was a member of Team USA in each of these three Olympic tournaments.

17. Name the Hall of Fame goaltender who refereed and coached in the National Hockey League.

Percy LeSueur was an outstanding goaltender in the pre-NHL era. LeSueur played for the Ottawa Senators, winning Stanley Cups in 1909, 1910 and 1911. He played his final two seasons with the Toronto Shamrocks and the Toronto Blue Shirts of the NHA, retiring in 1916. LeSueur later refereed and was the head coach of the NHL's Hamilton Tigers in 1923-24. The talented LeSueur was also the first manager of the Detroit Olympia, which was built in the late 1920s to house the new Detroit franchise in the National Hockey League. He was inducted into the Hall of Fame in 1961.

18. Name the two goaltenders who played in over fifty games and had a goals-against average of under 2.00 in the 2002-03 NHL season.

Marty Turco of the Dallas Stars and Roman Cechmanek of the Philadelphia Flyers both recorded goals-against averages under 2.00 in 2002-03. Turco's average of 1.72 in fifty-five games was the best since Davey Kerr's average of 1.54 in the 1939-40 season with the New York Rangers. Roman Cechmanek, who also had an outstanding year in 2002-03, recorded a goal-against average of 1.83 in fifty-eight games for the Philadelphia Flyers.

19. Name the only four American-born goaltenders who have won the Vezina Trophy.

Frank Brimsek was the first American-born Vezina winner. He was awarded the trophy in both 1938-39 and 1941-42 as a member of the Boston Bruins. It wasn't until 1983-84, when Tom Barrasso of the Buffalo Sabres won the Vezina, that a second American-born goalie was presented with the trophy. John Vanbiesbrouck of the New York Rangers was a winner in 1985-86 and Jim Carey of the Washington Capitals received the Vezina in 1995-96.

20. How many goalies have been selected number one overall in the NHL Entry Draft?

There have only been two goalies selected first in an NHL Entry Draft. Rick DiPietro was selected from Boston University first overall by the New York Islanders in the 2000 Entry Draft. Marc-Andre Fleury was also chosen first overall by the Pittsburgh Penguins from the Cape Breton Screaming Eagles of the Quebec Major Junior Hockey League in the 2003 Entry Draft.

Hall of Famers Johnny Bucyk and Jacques Plante faced each other in the 1970 Stanley Cup final.

PHOTO REPLAY

1. Name the three goaltenders who played for the St. Louis Blues in the 1970 final.

Jacques Plante, Ernie Wakely and Glenn Hall all played goal for the St. Louis Blues in the 1970 final. Jacques Plante started game one, but was badly injured on a Fred Stanfield slapshot early in the second period and was unable to play in the remainder of the series. Plante was replaced by Ernie Wakely with the score tied 1-1. The Bruins beat Wakely five times en route to a 6-1 victory. Wakely also played against the Bruins in the next match which the Bruins won 6-2. Glenn Hall was the St. Louis goaltender in the last two games of the series which the Bruins won by scores of 4-1 and 4-3. The fourth game was settled on Bobby Orr's famous overtime winner.

2. How many other NHL teams have had three goalies play in one Stanley Cup final series?

The 1928 New York Rangers and the 1938 Chicago Black Hawks both used three goalies when they captured the Cup in a final series. The Rangers' regular goalie, Lorne Chabot, went down with an injury in game two of the 1928 final. His replacement was Ranger coach and general manager Lester Patrick, who let in a single goal in the Rangers' 2-1 overtime win. The Rangers were allowed to use New York American goaltender Joe Miller for the remaining three games of the series against the Montreal Maroons. The Chicago Black Hawks' regular goaltender Mike Karakas was limited to games three and four of the 1938 final series against the Toronto Maple Leafs. Alfie Moore was loaned to the Black Hawks by the New York Americans as an emergency replacement for the injured Karakas in game one. When Moore defeated the Leafs 3-1 in the series opener, Toronto forced Chicago to use their own goaltender, Paul Goodman, from the Witchita Skyhawks of the American Hockey Association in game two, which Toronto took 5-1. Karakas returned to win both games three and four in the best-of-five final series.

3. When did Johnny Bucyk and Jacques Plante face each other in a Stanley Cup final prior to 1970?

Bucyk and Plante faced each other in a final on two previous occasions: in 1956 and 1958. In both cases, Plante tended goal for the Montreal Canadiens. In 1956, Bucyk was a member of the Detroit Red Wings and he skated with the Boston Bruins in 1958.

4. When were Bucyk and Plante teammates in the NHL?

Plante joined Bucyk on the Bruins briefly in 1973. Plante was traded by the Toronto Maple Leafs to the Boston Bruins in March of that year. He played eight games for the Bruins to close the regular season and was in goal for two playoff matches. Plante left the Bruins to become the general manager of the Quebec Nordiques of the WHA for the 1973-74 season.

For the Defense

In hockey, the reliability of the defense is critical. Both forwards and goaltenders depend on the defense to complement their positions. Throughout hockey's history, the significance of a strong defense can be seen by the contributions made to the game by players such as Eddie Shore, Doug Harvey, Bobby Orr and Ray Bourque. Today, players like Nicklas Lidstrom create a formidable barrier to the opponent's offense. Although the defensemen's skills are not always as spectacular as that of other players, the expertise they display in their position is key to the success of their team.

FIRST PERIOD - WHO AM I?

1. I am the only defenseman since Bobby Orr to have been awarded the Hart Trophy.

Chris Pronger of the St. Louis Blues was presented the Hart as league MVP for 1999-2000.

2. I prevented Ray Bourque from sweeping the Norris Trophy in five consecutive years.

Chris Chelios of the Montreal Canadiens was awarded the Norris Trophy in 1989. Boston Bruin Ray Bourque won the Norris in the two seasons prior to and following Chelios' win.

3. I was the highest scoring defenseman in the 2003 Stanley Cup playoffs.

Scott Niedermayer of the New Jersey Devils recorded eighteen points, with two goals and sixteen assists, in twenty-four games in the 2003 Stanley Cup playoffs. Niedermayer tied with teammate Jamie Langenbrunner for the overall lead in the playoff scoring race.

4. I was a member of a Stanley Cup-winning team in both Calgary and Montreal.

Rob Ramage was on the blue line with the Calgary Flames for the 1989 Stanley Cup win over the Montreal Canadiens. Ramage then played for the 1993 Stanley Cup winners in Montreal.

5. I am the only defenseman who was traded during the season and then named an NHL First All-Star member at the season's end.

Brad Park started the 1975-76 season as a member of the New York Rangers. He was traded to the Boston Bruins in November of 1975 and was later named to the First All-Star Team for that season.

6. I missed the playoffs in only one year of my twenty-one seasons in the NHL through 2002-03.

Scott Stevens has played in the Stanley Cup playoffs every year, aside from 1995-96, when the defending Stanley Cup champion Devils failed to qualify for post-season action.

7. In 1972-73, I played defense for both of the new NHL franchises.

Defenseman Arnie Brown had seen previous NHL action with the Maple Leafs, the Rangers and the Red Wings. He was traded by Detroit to the expansion New York Islanders in October of 1972. Brown played in forty-eight games with the Islanders before being dealt to their expansion cousin, the Atlanta Flames, in February of 1973. Brown skated in fifteen games with the Atlanta Flames that season. His final NHL season was 1973-74 when he played forty-eight games with the Flames before moving on for a single season in the WHA.

8. I was the leading scorer among defensemen on the New York Rangers in 2002-03.

Tom Poti recorded eleven goals and thirty-seven assists for forty-eight points in eighty games with the New York Rangers in 2002-03. The traditional scoring leader among the Rangers' defensemen, Brian Leetch, only recorded thirty points as his season was limited to fifty-one games due to injury.

9. I am the only player to be a member of the first Stanley Cup-winning team in both New Jersey and Dallas.

Shawn Chambers was a member of the 1995 New Jersey Devils and the 1999 Dallas Stars.

10. I was traded to the New York Rangers by the Colorado Rockies for five players in November of 1979.

Barry Beck was drafted second overall by the Colorado Rockies in the 1977 Amateur Draft. After an outstanding rookie season with the Rockies in 1977-78, his production tailed off and he was eventually traded to the New York Rangers. In return, the Rockies received Pat Hickey, Lucien DeBlois, Mike McEwen, Dean Turner and future considerations (Bobby Crawford). Beck played with the Rangers until retiring during the 1985-86 season. He returned for one season with the Los Angeles Kings in 1989-90.

11. I am the last defenseman to finish in the top ten in scoring in an NHL season.

Paul Coffey finished seventh overall in scoring in 1994-95, recording fourteen goals and forty-four assists for fifty-eight points, in the forty-five games he played in the lockout-shortened season. Coffey won the Norris Trophy for a third and final time during this season.

12. I was the first defenseman to record eight points in a single NHL game.

Tom Bladon of the Philadelphia Flyers recorded four goals and four assists in an 11-1 victory over the Cleveland Barons on December 11, 1977. Paul Coffey is the only other defenseman to ever record eight points in a single game, which he did on March 14, 1986, when Edmonton defeated Detroit 12-3.

13. I led the Washington Capitals in both the number of seasons and games played with the franchise, to the end of 2002-03.

Calle Johansson played in fifteen seasons with the Washington Capitals. In that time, he skated in 983 regular season and 95 playoff games with the franchise. Johansson announced his retirement from the NHL in the summer of 2003.

14. I led the Ottawa Senators in plus/minus rankings in the 2002-03 season.

The towering defenseman, Zdeno Chara, really came into his own for the Senators after arriving from the New York Islanders in a trade in June, 2001. Chara played his second solid season on the Senators' defense in 2002-03, recording a plus twenty-nine to lead all members of the team in this statistic.

15. I played defense for the Stanley Cup-winning New York Rangers in 1994 and Dallas Stars in 1999.

Sergei Zubov was playing in his second season with the Rangers, 1993-94, when his steady defensive play helped lead the club to their first Stanley Cup victory in fifty-four years. Zubov recorded nineteen points in twenty-two playoff games that year. Zubov was dealt to Pittsburgh in August of 1995. After a single season with the Penguins, he was traded to Dallas in June of 1996, where he played through the 2002-03 season. Zubov again put in a solid playoff appearance in 1999, anchoring the Dallas defense when they won the Cup.

16. I was traded in return for three first-round draft picks in August of 1994.

The Boston Bruins traded defenseman Glen Wesley to the Hartford Whalers in August of 1994, in exchange for Hartford's first round choices in the 1995, 1996 and 1997 Entry Drafts. During these drafts, Boston chose Kyle McLaren, Johnathan Aitken and Sergei Samsonov respectively. Wesley was in his ninth season with Hartford/Carolina when he was dealt to the Toronto Maple Leafs near the 2003 trading deadline. At season end, Wesley was an unrestricted free agent when he signed with the Carolina Hurricanes for the 2003-04 season.

17. I led the NHL in penalty minutes in the only two seasons I played in the league.

Hall of Fame defenseman "Bad Joe" Hall was a veteran with the Quebec Bulldogs of the NHA, when he joined the Montreal Canadiens for the inaugural NHL season in 1917-18. Hall recorded a league-leading 100 minutes in penalties that season and again topped the league with 89 minutes the following year. The Canadiens advanced to the 1919 Stanley Cup final against the Seattle Metropolitans, which was then cancelled due to the influenza epidemic which swept North America. Hall lost his life to the disease in a Seattle hospital on April 5, 1919.

18. I led the Ottawa Senators in scoring in their first NHL season of 1992-93.

Defenseman Norm Maciver scored seventeen goals and had forty-six assists for sixty-three points in the eighty games he played with the 1992-93 Ottawa Senators.

19. I am the only individual to have played on a Stanley Cup winner with both the Montreal Canadiens and the Philadelphia Flyers.

Ted Harris began his NHL career in Montreal, where he won the Stanley Cup in 1965, 1966, 1968 and 1969. He then moved on through Minnesota, Detroit and St. Louis before playing his final NHL season of 1974-75 with the Stanley Cup champion Philadelphia Flyers.

20. I hold the record for penalty minutes received in a single NHL game.

Randy Holt of the Los Angeles Kings received sixty-seven minutes in penalties in a game on March 11, 1979, when the Kings faced off against the Philadelphia Flyers. Holt received a minor penalty, three major penalties, two ten-minute misconducts and three game misconducts during the game. He recorded 1438 penalty minutes in 395 NHL regular season games with Chicago, Cleveland, Vancouver, Los Angeles, Calgary, Washington and Philadelphia in a career that spanned from 1974-75 through 1983-84.

SECOND PERIOD - MULTIPLE CHOICE

1. Which player was selected as an NHL First All-Star in his rookie season?

a) Ray Bourque   **b) Paul Coffey**
c) Doug Harvey   **d) Bobby Orr**

a) Ray Bourque was selected First Team All-Star in his rookie season of 1979-80, the only defenseman to achieve his amazing feat. Paul Coffey received the honor of Second Team All-Star in his second, third and fourth year in the league. He was named a First All-Star for the first time for his fifth NHL season. Doug Harvey's first selection to an NHL All-Star Team followed his fifth NHL season in 1951-52, when he was chosen as a First All-Star. Bobby Orr was a Second Team All-Star in his rookie season of 1966-67. He followed it up with eight consecutive selections to the First NHL All-Star Team, beginning in 1967-68.

2. How many defensemen have won the Norris Trophy as a New York Ranger?

a) 2   **b) 3**   **c) 4**   **d) 5**

b) 3. There have been three individuals win the Norris Trophy as a member of the Rangers. Doug Harvey was the first Ranger to have this honor in 1961-62. Harry Howell captured the Norris in 1966-67. Brian Leetch is the only other member of the Rangers to have been presented with the trophy. Leetch was selected the Norris winner in both 1991-92 and 1996-97.

3. How many times have both defensemen on the NHL First All-Star Team been members of the same franchise?

a) 3   **b) 6**   **c) 9**   **d) 12**

b) 6. There have been six occasions since the introduction of an annual First All-Star Team in 1930-31, where both defensemen honored have been regular season teammates.

Year	Defensemen	Team
1935-36	Eddie Shore, Babe Siebert	Boston Bruins
1938-39	Dit Clapper, Eddie Shore	Boston Bruins
1946-47	Butch Bouchard, Ken Reardon	Montreal Canadiens
1947-48	Bill Quackenbush, Jack Stewart	Detroit Red Wings
1948-49	Bill Quackenbush, Jack Stewart	Detroit Red Wings
2001-02	Chris Chelios, Nicklas Lidstrom	Detroit Red Wings

4. In how many NHL seasons was Bobby Orr able to play in every regular season game?

a) 0   **b) 1**   **c) 2**   **d) 3**

d) 3. Continually hampered by knee injuries throughout his short Hall of Fame career, Bobby Orr was only able to play in every regular season game on three different occasions. He participated in all seventy-six games of his fourth season in 1969-70. Again, in 1970-71, he played the entire season of seventy-eight games. Orr was also on the blueline in all eighty games in 1974-75, which was the last NHL season in which he could play more than twenty times.

5. Name the only year in which the first three selections at the NHL Entry Draft were all defensemen.

a) 1993   **b) 1994**   **c) 1995**   **d) 1996**

c) 1995. Bryan Berard, Wade Redden and Aki Berg were the top three selections respectively in the 1995 NHL Entry Draft. This is the only time that all of the top three selections in the draft were defensemen.

6. Which of these defensemen was selected to the most NHL First All-Star Teams, to the end of the 2002-03 season?

a) Rob Blake   **b) Sandis Ozolinsh**
c) Chris Pronger   **d) Scott Stevens**

d) Scott Stevens. Stevens was selected to the First All-Star Team in 1987-88 as a member of the Washington Capitals and again in 1993-94 as a member of the New Jersey Devils. The other three individuals have only had a single selection as a First Team All-Star. Sandis Ozolinsh with the Colorado Avalanche was chosen in 1996-97. Rob Blake was a member of the Los Angeles Kings in 1997-98 when he received the honor and Chris Pronger of the St. Louis Blues was selected in 1999-2000.

7. Which of the following defensemen is the oldest?

a) Chris Chelios   **b) Phil Housley**
c) Al MacInnis   **d) James Patrick**

a) Chris Chelios turned forty-one on January 25, 2003. Both Al MacInnis and James Patrick will have their fortieth birthday prior to the 2003-04 season, while Phil Housley will turn forty on March 9, 2004.

8. What is the highest number of consecutive seasons in which no defenseman was a repeat Norris Trophy winner?

a) 2   **b) 4**   **c) 6**   **d) 8**

d) 8. A different player was awarded the Norris Trophy as the NHL's top defenseman during each of the eight seasons between 1993-94 and 2000-01.

Season	Norris Trophy Winner	Team
1993-94	Ray Bourque	Boston Bruins
1994-95	Paul Coffey	Detroit Red Wings
1995-96	Chris Chelios	Chicago Blackhawks
1996-97	Brian Leetch	New York Rangers
1997-98	Rob Blake	Los Angeles Kings
1998-99	Al MacInnis	St. Louis Blues
1999-2000	Chris Pronger	St. Louis Blues
2000-01	Nicklas Lidstrom	Detroit Red Wings

9. Who holds the record for the most penalty minutes by a defenseman in a single NHL season?

a) Paul Baxter   **b) Steve Durbano**
c) Keith Magnuson   **d) Marty McSorley**

a) Paul Baxter recorded 409 penalty minutes in the 1981-82 season as a member of the Pittsburgh Penguins. This was the second highest total ever recorded by an NHL player at any position in a single season. Marty McSorley's highest penalty minute total for a season was 399 with the Los Angeles Kings in 1992-93. Steve Durbano recorded 370 minutes in the 1975-76 season, which he split between the Pittsburgh Penguins and the Kansas City Scouts. Keith Magnuson had 291 minutes in penalties for his highest total in the 1970-71 season with the Chicago Black Hawks.

10. How many times has a defenseman been named MVP at an NHL All-Star game?

a) 1　　　　**b) 2**　　　　**c) 3**　　　　**d) 4**

b) 2. Two defensemen, both representing the Boston Bruins, have been selected the most valuable player of an NHL All-Star game. The first was Bobby Orr, who played for the East Division All-Stars in the 25th Annual Game held in 1972. Ray Bourque was the only other defenseman to receive this honor when he was chosen MVP of the 1996 All-Star Game. These are the only two individuals to have been recognized as the MVP of an All-Star match as defensemen through the 2003 game.

11. Name the defenseman who has scored at least eighteen goals in each of the last five NHL seasons.

a) Rob Blake　　　　　　**b) Sergei Gonchar**
c) Nicklas Lidstrom　　　**d) Al MacInnis**

b) Sergei Gonchar of the Washington Capitals has scored goal totals of twenty-one, eighteen, nineteen, twenty-six and eighteen in the five seasons from 1998-99 through 2002-03.

12. Which player holds the NHL record for most goals by a rookie defenseman in one season?

a) Barry Beck　　　　**b) Phil Housley**
c) Reed Larson　　　　**d) Brian Leetch**

d) Brian Leetch scored twenty-three goals in his rookie season with the New York Rangers in 1988-89.

13. Who has participated in the most regular season games with the New York Rangers?

a) Ron Greschner　　　　**b) Harry Howell**
c) Brian Leetch　　　　　**d) Jim Neilson**

b) Harry Howell holds the mark having skated in 1160 regular season games with the club. Brian Leetch is second to Howell as the all-time leader in games played with the Rangers, having participated in 1072 games to the end of 2002-03. Greschner and Neilson currently rank fourth and eighth on the all-time list of games played as a Ranger.

14. Which defenseman recorded a point in the most consecutive games?

a) Ray Bourque **b) Paul Coffey**
c) Brian Leetch **d) Bobby Orr**

b) Paul Coffey received at least a point a game when he recorded sixteen goals and thirty-nine assists for fifty-five points over a twenty-eight game stretch, while playing with the Edmonton Oilers in 1985-86. Ray Bourque had a nineteen game streak with Boston in 1987-88. Brian Leetch, as a New York Ranger in 1991-92, scored a point in every game for a seventeen game stretch. Bobby Orr had a fifteen game point streak on two occasions, in 1970-71 and again in 1973-74.

15. Who was the leading scorer among defensemen at the 2002 Olympics?

a) Rob Blake **b) Phil Housley**
c) Nicklas Lidstrom **d) Brian Leetch**

c) Nicklas Lidstrom of Sweden scored one goal and recorded five assists for a total of six points in four games played with Sweden in the 2002 Olympics. Phil Housley and Brian Leetch led Team USA on defense with five points each in six games played, while Rob Blake was the leading defenseman in scoring on the Canadian Olympic team with one goal and two assists for three points.

16. Who was the captain of Team USA when they won the World Cup of Hockey in 1996?

a) Chris Chelios **b) Derian Hatcher**
c) Phil Housley **d) Brian Leetch**

d) Brian Leetch captained the winning American team in the 1996 World Cup. Leetch, along with Canada's Paul Coffey, recorded a tournament-leading seven assists during this event.

17. Who was the top plus/minus player in the 2003 NHL playoffs?

a) Keith Carney **b) Scott Niedermayer**
c) Sandis Ozolinsh **d) Scott Stevens**

d) Scott Stevens of the New Jersey Devils was a plus fourteen in his twenty-four playoff games with New Jersey in their Cup-winning season of 2003.

18. How many defensemen have won the Calder Trophy?

a) 9 **b) 10** **c) 11** **d) 12**

a) 9. There have been nine defensemen selected as the top rookie in the past seventy-one NHL seasons.

Player	Team	Season
Kent Douglas	Toronto Maple Leafs	1962-63
Jacques Laperriere	Montreal Canadiens	1963-64
Bobby Orr	Boston Bruins	1966-67
Denis Potvin	New York Islanders	1973-74
Ray Bourque	Boston Bruins	1979-80
Gary Suter	Calgary Flames	1985-86
Brian Leetch	New York Rangers	1988-89
Bryan Berard	New York Islanders	1996-97
Barret Jackman	St. Louis Blues	2002-03

19. Which defenseman was presented the Conn Smythe Trophy?

a) Ray Bourque **b) Paul Coffey**
c) Denis Potvin **d) Serge Savard**

d) Serge Savard. Savard is the only one of these outstanding defensemen to have been awarded the Conn Smythe as MVP in the playoffs. He won the Conn Smythe as a member of the Montreal Canadiens in 1969.

20. Which defenseman played the most NHL regular season games with a single franchise to the end of the 2002-03?

a) Ken Daneyko **b) Brian Leetch**
c) Bob Murray **d) Denis Potvin**

a) Ken Daneyko played in a total of 1283 games with the New Jersey Devils in his career which spanned from 1983-84 to 2002-03. Brian Leetch has participated in 1072 games with the New York Rangers to the end of the 2002-03 season. Denis Potvin was on the blueline in 1060 games with the New York Islanders, while Bob Murray played his 1008 games with the Chicago Blackhawks.

THIRD PERIOD - EXPERT TRIVIA

1. Name the first three individuals to win the James Norris Trophy while serving as captain of their team.

Doug Harvey, Pierre Pilote and Rod Langway. Doug Harvey won the Norris Trophy seven times in his career, but on only one occasion with Montreal in 1960-61 did he do so while being captain of the team. The next player to achieve this honor was Pierre Pilote, who was captain of the Chicago Black Hawks from 1961-62 through 1967-68 and earned three consecutive Norris wins from 1962-63 through 1964-65. The third captain to receive the Norris Trophy was Rod Langway of the Washington Capitals, who won his awards in his first two seasons as Washington's captain, 1982-83 and 1983-84.

2. Name the three defensemen who scored the most goals in the 2002-03 NHL season.

There were three defensemen who scored eighteen goals in the 2002-03 NHL season: Sergei Gonchar of the Washington Capitals, Nicklas Lidstrom of the Detroit Red Wings and Andy Delmore of the Nashville Predators.

3. Name the defensemen who were teammates on the Edmonton Oilers in the late 1990s and were reunited on the New York Islanders in 2003.

Roman Hamrlik and Janne Niinimaa were both traded to the Oilers in the 1997-98 season. Hamrlik arrived from Tampa Bay in December of 1997, while Niinimaa left Philadelphia in March of 1998. They were teammates in Edmonton until Hamrlik was traded to the Islanders in June of 2000. Niinimaa rejoined Hamrlik when he was dealt to the Islanders in March of 2003.

4. Name the only two defensemen to score for Team Canada during the 1972 Summit Series.

Brad Park and Bill White. The only goals from the defense came in game eight of the 1972 Summit Series. Brad Park tied the game at two with a goal late in the first period and Bill White evened the score at three midway through the second.

5. Which individual has played in the most seasons with the San Jose Sharks?

Mike Rathje finished his tenth season with the San Jose Sharks in 2002-03. He was selected third overall by San Jose in the 1992 Entry Draft and played his first game as a Shark in 1993-94. Since then, he has played in a total of 591 regular season and 54 playoff games with the franchise.

6. Where was Bill Barilko playing hockey before he skated with the Toronto Maple Leafs in 1946-47?

The Timmins, Ontario, native had been playing in the Pacific Coast Hockey League with the Hollywood Wolves for both 1945-46 and 1946-47. Barilko joined the Leafs and was part of the Cup-winning teams in 1947, 1948 and 1949. His Cup-winning goal in 1951 resulted in Toronto's fourth championship in his five seasons with the team.

7. Name the five defensemen who scored Stanley Cup-winning goals since Bill Barilko's overtime winner in 1951.

Montreal's J.C. Tremblay recorded the 1968 Cup-winning goal. Bobby Orr scored the Cup winner for the Boston Bruins in both 1970 and 1972. Paul Coffey netted the winner for the Edmonton Oilers against the Philadelphia Flyers in 1985. Pittsburgh Penguins' Ulf Samuelsson put the winner in Minnesota's net to capture the coveted trophy in 1991 and Uwe Krupp of the Colorado Avalanche scored the Cup-winning goal in the third overtime period in the 1996 Stanley Cup final against the Florida Panthers.

8. Name the four defensemen who were selected second overall in the NHL Entry Draft from 1993 to 1996.

Chris Pronger, Oleg Tverdovsky, Wade Redden and Andrei Zyuzin were all chosen second overall in the NHL Entry Draft in the years 1993 through 1996. Pronger was selected by the Hartford Whalers in 1993, after the Ottawa Senators had chosen Alexander Daigle. In 1994, Florida went with Ed Jovanovski as the first pick, with Tverdovsky coming second when he went to the Anaheim Mighty Ducks. The New York Islanders picked Wade Redden, following Ottawa's selection of Bryan Berard in the 1995 Draft. The 1996 Draft saw San Jose choose Zyuzin second overall, after Ottawa selected Chris Phillips first.

9. Name the five Toronto defensemen who have led the NHL in penalty minutes in a season.

Bill Barilko, Carl Brewer, Bert Corbeau, Red Horner and Gus Mortson have led the league in penalty minutes at the end of at least one season while playing with Toronto. Bert Corbeau was the first Toronto defenseman to do so with his 55 penalty minutes as a St. Pat in 1923-24. Carl Brewer is the most recent, as he finished the 1964-65 regular season with 177 penalty minutes on the Maple Leaf blueline. Red Horner holds the all-time mark as the penalty leader in eight straight NHL seasons, from 1932-33 to 1939-40.

10. Name the first player to be on four consecutive NHL Stanley Cup championship teams.

Hall of Fame defenseman Eddie Gerard of the Ottawa Senators was on the three Cup-winning teams of 1920, 1921 and 1923. The Senators were eliminated by the Toronto St. Pats in the 1922 playoffs. The St. Pats then went on to face the Vancouver Millionaires in the Stanley Cup final. The St. Pats, with Vancouver's permission, used Gerard as an emergency replacement due to injuries in game four of the 1922 Stanley Cup final. Toronto went on to defeat the Millionaires in the final, resulting in Gerard's name being engraved on the Cup in four consecutive years.

11. Name the only two players not born in Canada to have been awarded the Conn Smythe Trophy.

American-born Brian Leetch of the 1994 New York Rangers and Swedish-born Nicklas Lidstrom with the 2002 Detroit Red Wings are the only players not born in Canada to win the Conn Smythe Trophy.

12. Name the only defenseman to skate with the California/Oakland Seals and be inducted as a player into the Hockey Hall of Fame.

Harry Howell was a veteran of seventeen NHL seasons with the New York Rangers when he was dealt to the Oakland Seals in June of 1969. Howell played for his new team in 1969-70 and the first half of the following season. The franchise had now been renamed the California Golden Seals. He was dealt to the Los Angeles Kings in February of 1971. Howell finished his playing career in 1975-76 with the Calgary Cowboys of the WHA. He was inducted into the Hockey Hall of Fame in 1979.

13. Name the two defensemen whose junior careers both included a trip to the Memorial Cup and a selection to the 1982-83 Quebec Major Junior Hockey League All-Star Team. They both went on to lengthy NHL careers which saw them each play in five different Canadian NHL cities.

Bobby Dollas and Michel Petit. Bobby Dollas was a teammate of Mario Lemieux in Laval when the team made a trip to the Memorial Cup in 1984. He was selected fourteenth overall by the Winnipeg Jets in the 1983 Entry Draft and saw action through his sixteen season NHL career with several teams including Winnipeg, Quebec, Edmonton, Ottawa and Calgary. Petit attended the 1982 Memorial Cup as a member of the Sherbrooke Castors and was drafted by Vancouver eleventh overall in the 1982 draft. Petit saw action with ten different NHL clubs in a career which spanned sixteen seasons, through 1997-98. Five of those teams were located in the Canadian cities of Vancouver, Quebec, Toronto, Calgary and Edmonton.

14. Name the four defensemen with the highest point totals in the 2002-03 NHL season.

Highest Scoring Defensemen 2002-03

Player	Team	GP	G	A	PTS
Al MacInnis	St. Louis Blues	80	16	52	68
Sergei Gonchar	Washington Capitals	82	18	49	67
Nicklas Lidstrom	Detroit Red Wings	82	18	44	62
Sergei Zubov	Dallas Stars	82	11	44	55

15. What were Tim Horton's given names?

Tim Horton's actual name was Miles Gilbert Horton. Horton was killed in a car accident on February 21, 1974 in his twenty-fourth NHL season. He was an outstanding defenseman in the National Hockey League with the Toronto Maple Leafs, the New York Rangers, the Pittsburgh Penguins and the Buffalo Sabres. Tim Horton is probably better known today in association with the coffee and donut shops which bear his name.

16. Name the only two defensemen to have been selected to a WHA First All-Star Team on more than one occasion.

J.C. Tremblay of the Quebec Nordiques and Paul Shmyr of the Cleveland Crusaders were both selected to the First All-Star Team in the WHA for three separate seasons. Tremblay was chosen in 1972-73, 1974-75 and 1975-76, while Shmyr joined Tremblay on the First Team in 1972-73 and 1975-76. Shmyr was also selected a First All-Star in 1973-74.

17. Name the defenseman who was on the first Stanley Cup-winning team of both the New York Rangers and the Chicago Black Hawks.

Clarence "Taffy" Abel was a member of both the 1927-28 New York Rangers and the 1933-34 Chicago Black Hawks, the first time either one of these franchises won a Stanley Cup. Abel played for the Rangers for the first three seasons of their existence and finished his career as a member of the Chicago Black Hawks, winning the Cup in 1934.

18. Name the individual who was the highest scoring defenseman on the Nashville Predators in each of the last four seasons to the end of 2002-03.

Kimmo Timonen has been the leading scorer among defensemen on the Nashville Predators in each of the four seasons from 1999-2000 to 2002-03. Timonen most recently placed second in Predator scoring, with six goals and thirty-four assists for forty points in seventy-two games played during the 2002-03 season. His highest point total in a single season to date was in 2001-02, when he recorded forty-two points in eighty-two games.

19. Name the Canadian defense partners who were on the ice when Paul Henderson scored the winning goal in the 1972 Summit Series.

Bill White and Pat Stapleton were both on the ice when Henderson scored his winning goal with thirty-four seconds to go in game eight of the 1972 Summit Series. Several earlier accounts credited Serge Savard as being on the ice with Stapleton. However, more recently released footage of the series clearly shows Savard, heading off and being replaced by White, just prior to Henderson netting the winning goal behind Tretiak.

20. Who are the top five all-time point leaders among NHL defensemen?

Top Five Defensemen in Career Points (to the end of 2002-03 season)

Player	GP	G	A	PTS
Ray Bourque	1612	410	1169	1579
Paul Coffey	1409	396	1135	1531
Al MacInnis	1413	340	932	1272
Phil Housley	1495	338	894	1232
Larry Murphy	1615	287	929	1216

*Nicklas Lidstrom won the Norris Trophy for a third
consecutive season in 2002-03.*

PHOTO REPLAY

1. Name the three defensemen, prior to Nicklas Lidstrom, who have been presented with the Norris Trophy for at least three consecutive years.

Doug Harvey, Pierre Pilote and Bobby Orr. Montreal's Doug Harvey was awarded the Norris in four consecutive seasons from 1954-55 through 1957-58. Harvey had another run of Norris wins from 1959-60 through 1961-62, the last of these as a New York Ranger. Pierre Pilote of Chicago followed Harvey with three straight Norris-winning seasons from 1962-63 to 1964-65. Boston's Bobby Orr was awarded the Norris for eight consecutive years for his outstanding play from 1967-68 to 1974-75.

2. How many players have won the Norris Trophy as a member of the Detroit Red Wings?

Nicklas Lidstrom is the third Detroit defenseman to win the Norris Trophy. Red Kelly was the first recipient of the trophy in the 1953-54 season and Paul Coffey captured the honor on the Red Wing blue line in 1994-95.

3. Name the only defenseman, other than Nicklas Lidstrom, to average twenty-nine minutes of playing time per game in the 2002-03 NHL season.

Adrian Aucoin of the New York Islanders averaged twenty-nine minutes a game in the seventy-three games that he played with the team in 2002-03. Nicklas Lidstrom of the Detroit Red Wings was the leader in this category, averaging twenty-nine minutes and twenty seconds, while appearing in eighty-two games.

4. How many NHL teams have retired sweater number 5 to honor a defenseman?

Four teams have retired sweater number 5 to honor an outstanding defenseman. The Boston Bruins (Dit Clapper), the Toronto Maple Leafs (Bill Barilko), the New York Islanders (Denis Potvin) and the Washington Capitals (Rod Langway) have all retired this sweater number.

Fast Forward

Being a forward is a high-profile position. Goal scorers get noticed! The red light goes on and the crowd rises. The images of end-to-end rushes by Rocket Richard, Bobby Hull and Guy Lafleur are forever etched in the hockey fan's mind. Gretzky and Lemieux turned the hockey world upside down with their amazing talent and finesse. But forwards do more than score goals. Gordie Howe, a significant scoring threat, was also known as a skilled two-way forward; a role exemplified by Peter Forsberg in the NHL today. Being a complete forward consists of more than putting the puck in the net.

FIRST PERIOD - WHO AM I?

1. I was the runner-up in the scoring race for the Art Ross Trophy in both 2001-02 and 2002-03.

Markus Naslund of the Vancouver Canucks finished second in points to Jarome Iginla of the Calgary Flames in 2001-02. Naslund was the scoring leader near the end of the 2002-03 season, but was passed by Peter Forsberg of the Colorado Avalanche on the last day of the schedule.

2. I am the only forward to be named to the NHL First All-Star Team in my rookie season.

Teemu Selanne of the Winnipeg Jets was selected First Team All-Star at right wing in his rookie year of 1992-93. Selanne also picked up the Calder Trophy as he recorded an amazing seventy-six goals that season.

3. I finished ahead of Gordie Howe in scoring in each of the five seasons between 1957-58 and 1961-62.

New York Ranger Andy Bathgate finished ahead of Gordie Howe of the Detroit Red Wings in scoring in these five consecutive seasons. Both of these right wingers were dominant forces at the time. Howe won the Art Ross Trophy in 1956-57 and would repeat the honor in 1962-63, but Bathgate stayed ahead of him in the NHL scoring race in each of the seasons between.

4. I am the only player to win a Stanley Cup with both the New York Islanders and the New York Rangers.

Greg Gilbert was a member of the Stanley Cup-winning New York Islanders in his first two seasons with the team in 1981-82 and 1982-83. He was traded to the Chicago Blackhawks in 1989. Gilbert then signed as a free agent with the Rangers for their Cup-winning 1993-94 season. He skated with the St. Louis Blues in the next two seasons before retiring.

5. I achieved the highest penalty minute total ever for the leading scorer in my Art Ross Trophy-winning season.

Stan Mikita of the Chicago Black Hawks earned the Art Ross Trophy in 1964-65 by scoring twenty-eight goals and adding fifty-nine assists for eighty-seven points in a seventy-game schedule. Mikita accumulated 154 penalty minutes that season. Mikita cleaned up his game while leading the scoring race again in both 1966-67 and 1967-68. He added the Lady Byng Trophy for both of these seasons when he reduced his penalty minute totals to twelve and fourteen respectively.

6. I am the only individual to skate on three Olympic medal-winning teams as well as three Stanley Cup winners.

Igor Larionov won gold medals with the Soviet Union in both the 1984 and 1988 Winter Olympics and was a member of the bronze-winning Russian squad at the 2002 tournament in Salt Lake City. Larionov also skated with the Detroit Red Wing teams that won the Stanley Cup in 1997, 1998 and 2002.

7. I was the highest playoff scorer to not advance to the Stanley Cup final in 2003.

Marian Gaborik of the Minnesota Wild recorded seventeen points, with nine goals and eight assists, in the eighteen games he played in the 2003 playoffs. Gaborik's Minnesota Wild were eliminated by the Anaheim Mighty Ducks in the Western Conference final. Gaborik finished only a single point behind playoff scoring leaders Jamie Langenbrunner and Scott Niedermayer of the New Jersey Devils.

8. I was suspended for twenty games early in the 1983-84 NHL season for intentionally tripping a linesman.

Tom Lysiak of the Chicago Black Hawks intentionally tripped linesman Ron Foyt during a game played on October 30, 1983. This action resulted in a twenty game suspension. Lysiak entered the season having scored more than twenty goals in each of nine straight seasons. His production dropped off to just seventeen goals in the fifty-four games he was able to play in 1983-84. His scoring touch never came back to its previous level and he played his last NHL game in 1986 with Chicago.

9. I was selected MVP of the 2003 NHL All-Star Game.

Dany Heatley of the Atlanta Thrashers was named MVP when he recorded four goals in his first NHL All-Star game, which was held on Sunday, February 2, 2003, in Sunrise, Florida. Heatley added a fifth goal for the East in the shoot-out, which was used following overtime to break the tied game. Heatley's extra marker was not sufficient to defeat the West who won 6-5.

10. I was the first player to score an overtime winner in an NHL All-Star game.

Gilbert Perreault of the Buffalo Sabres scored the winning goal for the Wales Conference at 3:55 of overtime in the 31st NHL All-Star Game. The match was held on January 24, 1978, appropriately at the Buffalo Memorial Auditorium where Perreault played for the Sabres. Steve Shutt and Borje Salming drew assists on the play which resulted in a 3-2 win. Perreault beat Philadelphia goaltender Wayne Stephenson, who was in net for the Campbell Conference All-Stars.

11. I was the highest scorer to split the 2002-03 season between two NHL teams.

Alexei Kovalev earned sixty-four points in fifty-four games with the Penguins before being traded to the Rangers where he recorded another thirteen points over twenty-four games. His seventy-seven points placed him nineteenth in league scoring for 2002-03.

12. I led the Toronto Maple Leafs in scoring for the most consecutive seasons.

Mats Sundin led the Leafs in scoring in every one of his first eight seasons with the team from 1994-95 through 2001-02. Alexander Mogilny was the Leafs' leading scorer for the 2002-03 season.

13. I am a power forward who has been an NHL regular since 1992-93. While I averaged fifty points in each of my first eleven NHL seasons, I only recorded half that number in the year I won the Stanley Cup.

Bill Guerin was a member of the 1995 New Jersey Devils, the only year he has won the Cup to date. He recorded twenty-five points in forty-eight games in a lockout-shortened season.

14. I am the only player to be on six Stanley Cup winners during the 1960s.

Dick Duff was a member of the Toronto Maple Leaf Stanley Cup winners in 1961-62 and 1962-63. He was traded to the New York Rangers in the blockbuster deal involving Andy Bathgate in February of 1964. The Rangers then traded him to Montreal in December of 1964, where he went on to win the Cup with the Canadiens in 1965, 1966, 1968 and 1969.

15. I was credited with the goal that eliminated the Edmonton Oilers from the 1986 playoffs.

Perry Berezan was credited with the goal that Edmonton defenseman Steve Smith banged in off goaltender Grant Fuhr, as the Edmonton Oilers' "own goal" eliminated them from the 1986 playoffs. The goal at 5:14 of the third period gave the Calgary Flames a 3-2 win in the seventh game of the Smythe Division final. It marked the only time between 1984 and 1988 that Edmonton did not win the Stanley Cup. The Flames advanced to the Cup final, only to be defeated by the Montreal Canadiens in five games.

16. I scored the fastest two goals by one player in NHL playoff history.

Norm Ullman of the Detroit Red Wings scored two goals five seconds apart in a 1965 semi-final game against the Chicago Black Hawks. Ullman scored on Chicago's Glenn Hall at 17:35 and 17:40 of the second period in game five, which Detroit went on to win 4-2. Unfortunately for the Red Wings, Chicago won the best-of-seven series four games to three.

17. I had scored 276 goals over eight NHL regular seasons before I finally participated in a playoff game in 1983.

For eight seasons, high-scoring centre Dennis Maruk had outstanding offensive numbers with some of the NHL's weaker teams before he finally participated in his first playoff action as a member of the Washington Capitals in 1983.

Denis Maruk's First Eight NHL Seasons

Year	Team	GP	G	A	PTS
1975-76	California	80	30	32	62
1976-77	Cleveland	80	28	50	78
1977-78	Cleveland	76	36	35	71
1978-79	Minnesota	20	0	0	0
	Washington	76	31	59	90
1979-80	Washington	27	10	17	27
1980-81	Washington	80	50	47	97
1981-82	Washington	80	60	76	136
1982-83	Washington	80	31	50	81

Maruk went on to play with the Minnesota North Stars for six more NHL seasons and saw further playoff appearances in three of those.

18. I am the all-time leading scorer in Canada Cup/World Cup tournaments.

Wayne Gretzky scored twenty goals and forty-four assists for a total of sixty-four points in Canada Cup/World Cup tournaments. Gretzky played in a total of thirty-nine games in the five tournaments held between 1981 and 1996.

19. I played for the Florida Panthers and the Anaheim Mighty Ducks in different Stanley Cup final series.

Rob Niedermayer was in his third season as a member of the Florida Panthers when the team went to the Stanley Cup final in 1996, against the eventual champion Colorado Avalanche. He played in eight seasons with Florida before being dealt to the Calgary Flames in June of 2001. Niedermayer was traded to Anaheim in March of 2003, and was an important member of the Mighty Ducks when they took New Jersey to seven games in the 2003 Stanley Cup final.

20. My first NHL playoff goal was the Stanley Cup winner in 2003.

Mike Rupp scored his first NHL playoff goal to give the New Jersey Devils a 1-0 lead in the seventh game of the 2003 Stanley Cup final. Rupp added two assists in the Devils' 3-0 victory over Anaheim in the deciding game.

SECOND PERIOD - MULTIPLE CHOICE

1. Which player scored the only goal for the Minnesota Wild in the 2003 Western Conference final?

a) Andrew Brunette   b) Marian Gaborik

c) Wes Walz   d) Sergei Zholtok

a) Andrew Brunette scored the lone Wild goal, in Minnesota's 2-1 loss to Anaheim, in the last game of the Western Conference final on May 16, 2003. The Wild had been held scoreless in the first three games of this series.

2. Who was the last player to lead the Stanley Cup playoffs in scoring for three consecutive seasons?

a) Wayne Gretzky   b) Guy Lafleur

c) Mario Lemieux   d) Bryan Trottier

a) Wayne Gretzky led the playoff scoring race for three consecutive years from 1983 through 1985. Gretzky was also the leading scorer in the playoffs on three other occasions in 1987, 1988 and 1993. Lafleur led or tied for the lead for the three years from 1977 through 1979, while Lemieux was the playoff scoring leader in 1991 and 1992. Trottier led the playoff scoring race in 1980 and 1982.

3. Which player scored twenty or more goals in every one of his NHL seasons?

a) **Mike Gartner** b) **Jacques Lemaire**
c) **Gilbert Perreault** d) **Jean Pronovost**

b) Jacques Lemaire scored twenty or more goals in each of his twelve NHL seasons between 1967-68 to 1978-79. Mike Gartner scored more than thirty goals in seventeen of his nineteen seasons in the league. There were, however, two times he didn't reach twenty goals. Gilbert Perreault of the Buffalo Sabres scored twenty or more goals in fifteen of his seventeen seasons. For twelve of his fourteen NHL seasons, Jean Pronovost reached the twenty-goal mark.

4. Which player did not lead his team in scoring in the 2002-03 season?

a) **Sergei Fedorov** b) **Paul Kariya**
c) **Todd Marchant** d) **Teemu Selanne**

c) Todd Marchant of the Edmonton Oilers finished the 2002-03 season with sixty points. Ryan Smyth narrowly beat him as team scoring leader with sixty-one points. Fedorov, Kariya and Selanne led Detroit, Anaheim and San Jose respectively in team scoring in 2002-03. All four of these players will start the 2003-04 season with new clubs, signed on as free agents. Fedorov has gone to Anaheim; Marchant is now with Columbus; and Kariya and Selanne are on the Colorado Avalanche.

5. Which player recorded fewer regular season points in the 2002-03 season than in 2001-02?

a) **Jason Blake** b) **Marian Gaborik**
c) **Olli Jokinen** d) **Vincent Lecavalier**

b) Marian Gaborik had an amazing 2003 playoff season, recording seventeen points in eighteen games. However, his regular season scoring totals actually dropped slightly from the previous year. Gaborik recorded sixty-seven points in seventy-eight games with Minnesota in 2001-02, but dropped marginally to sixty-five points in eighty-one games with the 2002-03 Minnesota Wild. The other three players showed dramatic point increases, from 2001-02 to 2002-03. Jason Blake of the New York Islanders improved from eighteen points to fifty-five points. Panther Olli Jokinen increased his total points from twenty-nine to sixty-five and Vincent Lecavalier of the Tampa Bay Lightning shot up from thirty-seven points to seventy-eight points over the two seasons.

6. Which player participated in the Olympic games on three occasions?

a) Paul Kariya   b) Eric Lindros
c) Joe Nieuwendyk   d) Brendan Shanahan

b) Eric Lindros skated with the Canadian Olympic team in 1992, 1998 and 2002. The other three players have all seen action on the Canadian Olympic team on two occasions. Kariya played in 1994 and 2002, while both Nieuwendyk and Shanahan participated in both the 1998 and 2002 Winter Olympic Games.

7. Which player has never led the Atlanta Thrashers in scoring for an NHL season?

a) Andrew Brunette   b) Ray Ferraro
c) Dany Heatley   d) Iyla Kovalchuk

d) Iyla Kovalchuk has never led Atlanta in scoring for a season. Andrew Brunette led with fifty points in the eighty-one games he played with the Thrashers in their first season of 1999-2000. The following year, Ray Ferraro led the way with seventy-six points in eighty-one games played. Dany Heatley has led the scoring for the Atlanta Thrashers for the past two seasons, recording sixty-seven points in eighty-two games in his rookie season of 2001-02 and improving that record to eighty-nine points in seventy-seven games played in 2002-03. Kovalchuk has finished second and third in the Thrashers' scoring in his first two seasons with the team.

8. Who was the first player to score fifty goals in a season with the Minnesota North Stars?

a) Brian Bellows

b) Dino Ciccarelli

c) Mike Modano

d) Steve Payne

b) Dino Ciccarelli hit the fifty-goal plateau on two occasions as a member of the Minnesota North Stars. The first time was in 1981-82, when he recorded fifty-five goals. Ciccarelli had a second season reaching the fifty-goal mark in 1986-87, when he recorded fifty-two goals. Brian Bellows and Mike Modano are the only other players from this franchise who have reached fifty goals in a season. Bellows scored fifty-five goals while playing with the North Stars in 1989-90. Modano hit fifty goals in 1993-94, the first season after the team relocated to Dallas. Steve Payne put up some impressive numbers in his ten seasons on left wing with the North Stars, but his highest goal-scoring total was forty-two in 1979-80.

9. How many times have teammates both scored sixty or more goals in the same NHL season?

a) 1

b) 2

c) 3

d) 4

b) 2. The first teammates to accomplish this were Wayne Gretzky and Jari Kurri with the 1984-85 Edmonton Oilers. Gretzky recorded 73 goals, while Kurri scored 71 in that season. The only other teammates to achieve this feat were Mario Lemieux and Jaromir Jagr of the Pittsburgh Penguins, who recorded 69 and 62 goals respectively in 1995-96.

10. Who is the last individual to lead the NHL in penalty minutes for two consecutive seasons?

a) Matthew Barnaby

b) Tim Hunter

c) Chris Nilan

d) Rob Ray

c) Chris Nilan led the league in penalty minutes as a member of the Montreal Canadiens in both 1983-84 and 1984-85, recording 338 and 358 minutes in the box for those respective seasons. The other three players have all led the NHL in penalty minutes for two separate, but not consecutive, seasons since 1985.

11. How many players were teammates while winning the Stanley Cup with both the Dallas Stars in 1999 and the New Jersey Devils in 2003?

a) 2   b) 3   c) 4   d) 5

b) 3. Jamie Langenbrunner, Grant Marshall and Joe Nieuwendyk were all members of both of these Stanley Cup-winning teams.

12. Which player has competed in only one Olympic competition for Sweden?

a) Daniel Alfredsson   b) Peter Forsberg
c) Markus Naslund   d) Mats Sundin

c) Markus Naslund's only Olympic appearance was at the 2002 Winter Games. Alfredsson and Sundin competed for Sweden in both the 1998 and 2002 Games. Peter Forsberg, recovering from injuries, was forced to miss the 2002 competition. He had competed for Sweden in both the 1994 and 1998 Olympics.

13. How many players have won the Frank J. Selke Trophy on three or more occasions?

a) 1   b) 2   c) 3   d) 4

c) 3. Montreal's Bob Gainey won the Selke Trophy for the first four years it was awarded from 1978 to 1981. Guy Carboneau, another Canadien, was presented with the trophy in 1988, 1989 and again in 1992. The most recent player to win a third Selke was Jere Lehtinen of the Dallas Stars, who received the award in 1998, 1999 and again in 2003.

14. Who was the first individual to be named MVP of two NHL All-Star games?

a) Wayne Gretzky   b) Bobby Hull
c) Mario Lemieux   d) Frank Mahovlich

d) Frank Mahovlich was named the most valuable player of the All-Star match in both 1963 and 1969. He received the honor in 1963, as a member of the Stanley Cup-winning Toronto Maple Leafs. He was MVP again in 1969, representing the Detroit Red Wings on the Eastern Division All-Stars. Bobby Hull was the first to win back-to-back MVPs as an All-Star which he did in 1970 and 1971. Both Wayne Gretzky and Mario Lemieux have won the award on three occasions.

15. Which individual is the career leader in playoff power-play goals?

a) Mike Bossy   b) Dino Ciccarelli
c) Wayne Gretzky   d) Brett Hull

d) Brett Hull has scored thirty-seven power-play goals in the playoffs, to the end of 2003. Bossy recorded thirty-five over his career, while both Ciccarelli and Gretzky had thirty-four career playoff power-play goals.

16. Who holds the record for the most assists in one period of an NHL game?

a) Marcel Dionne   b) Ron Francis
c) Dale Hawerchuk   d) Steve Yzerman

c) Dale Hawerchuk recorded five assists in the second period of a 7-3 Winnipeg victory at Los Angeles on March 6, 1984.

17. Which player led his team in scoring by the widest margin in the 2002-03 season?

a) Pavol Demitra   b) Mike Modano
c) Mario Lemieux   d) Ziggy Palffy

d) Ziggy Palffy led the Los Angeles Kings with eighty-five points in 2002-03. Teammate Jaroslav Modry finished with thirty-eight points, a distant second, lagging forty-seven points behind Palffy. Mario Lemieux came close to Palffy's mark, leading teammate Martin Straka by a forty-five point margin. Mike Modano was thirty points ahead of teammate Sergei Zubov and Pavol Demitra led teammate Al MacInnis with a twenty-five point spread.

18. Who holds the record for the most points in a season as a member of the Minnesota Wild?

a) Andrew Brunette   b) Pascal Dupuis
c) Marian Gaborik   d) Cliff Ronning

a) Andrew Brunette led the Minnesota Wild in scoring with sixty-nine points in eighty-one games played in the 2001-02 season, the highest point total by any member of the Wild over their first three NHL seasons.

19. Which individual was the leading point-getter for the Tampa Bay Lightning in 2002-03?

a) Vincent Lecavalier   b) Vaclav Prospal

c) Brad Richards   d) Martin St. Louis

b) Vaclav Prospal led Tampa Bay in scoring in 2002-03. He moved on to Anaheim as a free agent in July of 2003.

Tampa Bay Lightning Highest Scorers 2002-03

Name	GP	G	A	PTS
Vaclav Prospal	80	22	57	79
Vincent Lecavalier	80	33	45	78
Brad Richards	80	17	57	74
Martin St. Louis	82	33	37	70

20. How many players have scored at least seventy goals in an NHL season?

a) 6   b) 8   c) 10   d) 12

b) 8. Wayne Gretzky leads the way, having accomplished this feat on four separate occasions in the seasons between 1981-82 and 1984-85. Brett Hull also reached this plateau in three consecutive seasons from 1989-90 through 1991-92. Mario Lemieux hit the mark in 1987-88 and again in 1988-89. Five more players who have reached the seventy-goal plateau in one NHL season are: Phil Esposito, Jari Kurri, Bernie Nicholls, Alexander Mogilny and Teemu Selanne.

THIRD PERIOD - EXPERT TRIVIA

1. Name the three players who finished in the top ten in points for both the 2001-02 and 2002-03 NHL seasons.

Markus Naslund and Todd Bertuzzi of the Vancouver Canucks, along with Pavol Demitra of the St. Louis Blues, are the only individuals to be top ten scorers in both of these seasons.

2. Name the top three rookies in scoring in the 2002-03 NHL season.

Player	Team	GP	G	A	PTS
Henrik Zetterberg	Detroit	79	22	22	44
Tyler Arnason	Chicago	82	19	20	39
Rick Nash	Columbus	74	17	22	39

3. Name the first four players to have scored sixty goals in an NHL regular season.

Phil Esposito of the Boston Bruins was the first to achieve this feat. He attained sixty goals in four seasons before anyone else reached this mark. Esposito scored seventy-six goals in 1970-71; sixty-six in 1971-72; sixty-eight in 1973-74; and sixty-one in 1974-75. Reggie Leach of the Philadelphia Flyers was next, scoring sixty-one goals in the 1975-76 season. Steve Shutt of the Montreal Canadiens followed in 1976-77, when he scored sixty goals. Guy Lafleur, also as a Canadien, scored sixty goals the following season, 1977-78.

4. Name the four teams Dale Hawerchuk played on during his NHL career.

Dale Hawerchuk played for the Winnipeg Jets, the Buffalo Sabres, the St. Louis Blues and the Philadelphia Flyers during his sixteen-year NHL career. He scored forty or more goals in seven of his nine seasons with the Winnipeg Jets before being traded to Buffalo in 1990. Hawerchuk put in five seasons with Buffalo before signing as a free agent with St. Louis in September of 1995. He was then traded to Philadelphia in March of 1996, where he continued to play until his retirement in 1997. Hawerchuk was inducted into the Hockey Hall of Fame in 2001.

5. Who was the all-time franchise leader in goals, assists and points for the Houston Aeros of the WHA?

Larry Lund played six solid seasons in the World Hockey Association for the Houston Aeros. Lund appeared in 459 games, recording 149 goals and 277 assists for 426 points, making him the all-time leader in goals, assists and points for the franchise. He also recorded 65 points in 59 playoff games with the Aeros. He was the playoff leader with 23 points in 1974, the year of the Aeros' first WHA championship. Lund did not play a single game in the NHL.

6. Name the oldest two individuals who played during the 2002-03 NHL season.

Igor Larionov of the Detroit Red Wings and Mark Messier of the New York Rangers both turned forty-two during the 2002-03 season. Larionov celebrated his forty-second birthday on December 3, 2002, while Messier turned forty-two on January 18, 2003.

7. Name the two members of the New Jersey Devils who each had four game-winning goals in the 2003 Stanley Cup playoffs.

Both Jamie Langenbrunner and Jeff Friesen recorded four game-winning goals for the New Jersey Devils in the 2003 Stanley Cup playoffs.

8. When was the first time there were four different winners of the Art Ross Trophy in four consecutive seasons?

The Art Ross Trophy was first awarded to the leading scorer of the NHL for the 1947-48 season. In the first four seasons that the trophy was awarded, it was presented to four different players.

Art Ross Trophy Winners

Year	Player	Team	GP	G	A	PTS
1947-48	Elmer Lach	Montreal	60	30	31	61
1948-49	Roy Conacher	Chicago	60	26	42	68
1949-50	Ted Lindsay	Detroit	69	23	55	78
1950-51	Gordie Howe	Detroit	70	43	43	86

The most recent time that the Art Ross Trophy was presented to four different players in four consecutive seasons occurred from 1977-78 to 1980-81. For those years, Guy Lafleur of the Montreal Canadiens, Bryan Trottier of the New York Islanders, Marcel Dionne of the Los Angeles Kings and Wayne Gretzky of the Edmonton Oilers were the recipients. Recently, Peter Forsberg's Art Ross win in 2002-03 marked the third player in three consecutive years to receive the honor.

9. Who was the leading scorer at the 2003 Memorial Cup Tournament held in Quebec City?

Gregory Campbell of the tournament-winning Kitchener Rangers recorded one goal and six assists for seven points in four games at the 2003 Memorial Cup championship. Campbell is the son of former NHL player and coach, Colin Campbell, who has served as an executive vice president of the league since 1998. Gregory Campbell was selected by the Florida Panthers as the 67th choice overall in the 2002 Entry Draft. He was also a member of the Canadian silver medal-winning team at the 2003 World Junior Championship.

10. Who holds the record, along with Wayne Gretzky, for the most assists in one NHL game?

Billy Taylor of the Detroit Red Wings recorded seven assists on March 16, 1947, when his Red Wings defeated the Black Hawks by a score of 10-6. Wayne Gretzky equaled this mark of seven assists in a single game on three occasions in the 1980s as a member of the Edmonton Oilers.

11. Name the only member of the Washington Capitals who led the NHL in goal scoring in a single season.

Peter Bondra has twice been the top goal scorer in an NHL season. Bondra led the league in the lockout-shortened 1994-95 season with thirty-four goals. He then tied with Teemu Selanne for the lead when they both scored fifty-two goals in 1997-98.

12. When was the last time there were no duplicated players in the top five scorers in consecutive NHL seasons?

The 1993-94 and 1994-95 seasons each saw five different individuals lead the scoring race.

Leading Scorers 1993-94

Player	Team	GP	G	A	PTS
Wayne Gretzky	Los Angeles	81	38	92	130
Sergei Fedorov	Detroit	82	56	64	120
Adam Oates	Boston	77	32	80	112
Doug Gilmour	Toronto	83	27	84	111
Pavel Bure	Vancouver	76	60	47	107

Leading Scorers 1994-95

Player	Team	GP	G	A	PTS
Jaromir Jagr	Pittsburgh	48	32	38	70
Eric Lindros	Philadelphia	46	29	41	70
Alexei Zhamnov	Winnipeg	48	30	35	65
Joe Sakic	Quebec	47	19	43	62
Ron Francis	Pittsburgh	44	11	48	59

13. Name the three forwards for the 1974-75 Montreal Canadiens who entered the 2003-04 season as general managers of an NHL team.

General managers Bob Gainey (Montreal Canadiens), Doug Risebrough (Minnesota Wild) and Glen Sather (New York Rangers) were all teammates on the 1974-75 Montreal Canadiens.

14. Name the only franchise to have had four brothers play in the NHL with that organization.

Four of the six Sutter brothers played on the Chicago Blackhawks at some point in their career. Darryl skated his entire NHL career for Chicago, from 1979-80 to 1986-87. Duane played his last three NHL seasons as a Blackhawk, coming over from the Islanders in 1987. Brent was traded from the Islanders to the Blackhawks in 1991 and remained there through the end of his career in 1998. Rich was a member of the Blackhawks for 1993-94 and began the following season with them, before being traded to Tampa Bay. Only Brian and Ron Sutter never saw any game action with the Chicago Blackhawks, however, Brian is now head coach of the team.

15. Were there more players with a left-hand shot or a right-hand shot in the top ten scorers for the 2002-03 NHL season?

Seven of the ten top scorers in the 2002-03 NHL season shot left.

NHL Top Scorers 2002-03

Player	Team	Points	Shoots
Peter Forsberg	Colorado	106	Left
Markus Naslund	Vancouver	104	Left
Joe Thornton	Boston	101	Left
Milan Hejduk	Colorado	98	Right
Todd Bertuzzi	Vancouver	97	Left
Pavol Demitra	St. Louis	93	Left
Glen Murray	Boston	92	Right
Mario Lemieux	Pittsburgh	91	Right
Dany Heatley	Atlanta	89	Left
Ziggy Palffy	Los Angeles	85	Left

16. Which team scoring leader had the lowest point total in the 2002-03 NHL season?

David Legwand of the Nashville Predators had 48 points in 64 games to lead his team in scoring in 2002-03. The next lowest team leader had 57 points in 81 games. This was recorded by Patrick Elias of the Stanley Cup champion New Jersey Devils.

17. Name the four European-born players with the highest point totals for any single NHL season.

Player	Year	Team	GP	G	A	PTS
Jaromir Jagr	1995-96	Pittsburgh Penguins	82	62	87	149
Peter Stastny	1981-82	Quebec Nordiques	80	46	93	139
Jari Kurri	1984-85	Edmonton Oilers	73	71	64	135
Teemu Selanne	1992-93	Winnipeg Jets	84	76	56	132

18. Name the only two players, other than Bobby Hull, to score fifty goals as a Chicago Blackhawk in a single NHL season.

Al Secord and Jeremy Roenick each scored fifty goals in an NHL season as Blackhawks. While Bobby Hull had five seasons in which he scored fifty goals or more, Blackhawk fans have seen few fifty-goal seasons by a player since then. Al Secord was the next Chicago skater to follow Hull's feat, when he recorded fifty-four goals in the 1982-83 season. Jeremy Roenick then scored fifty-three goals in 1991-92 and followed it up with fifty goals in 1992-93.

19. Name the only two players to score at least forty goals in both the 2001-02 and 2002-2003 NHL seasons.

Player	Goals in 2001-02	Goals in 2002-03
Glen Murray	41	44
Markus Naslund	40	48

20. How many times have all three forwards on the NHL First All-Star Team played for the same franchise?

There have been four seasons in which all three First Team All-Star forwards played for the same NHL team. The first time this happened was in 1944-45 when the "Punch" line of Elmer Lach at center, Maurice "Rocket" Richard at right wing and Toe Blake at left wing all represented the Montreal Canadiens. In both 1963-64 and 1966-67, three Chicago forwards were named to the First All-Star Team: Stan Mikita at center, Kenny Wharram at right wing and Bobby Hull at left wing. The most recent case occurred in 1970-71, when Boston Bruins made up the All-Star forward line of Phil Esposito at center, Ken Hodge at right wing and Johnny Bucyk at left wing.

Two of hockey's greatest stars, Mario Lemieux and Mark Messier, were still playing in the 2002-03 season.

PHOTO REPLAY

1. Name the only captain of a Stanley Cup winner, other than Mario Lemieux or Mark Messier, between 1990 and 1994.

Guy Carbonneau was captain of the Cup-winning Montreal Canadiens in 1993. Messier held the captaincy for the Oilers in 1990 and the Rangers in 1994, when these teams were champions. Lemieux captained the 1991 and 1992 Pittsburgh Penguins during their successful bids for the Cup.

2. Name the only player, other than Mark Messier or Mario Lemieux, to win the Hart Trophy in the four seasons between 1989-90 and 1992-93.

Brett Hull of the St. Louis Blues was awarded the Hart Trophy for the 1990-91 season. Messier won the trophy as a member of the Oilers in 1990 and again with the Rangers in 1992. Lemieux received the Hart in 1993. He had previously received the honor in 1988 and would win it again in 1996.

3. Which player, Mario Lemieux or Mark Messier, has been selected to the NHL First All-Star Team on the most occasions?

Mario Lemieux has been selected to the NHL First All-Star Team five times, while Messier has been selected on four occasions.

4. Name the only three players, other than Mark Messier, to be named to the NHL All-Star Team at two different forward positions.

Sid Abel was named as a Second Team All-Star in the 1941-42 season as a left winger. Abel was also the First Team center in both 1948-49 and 1949-50 and the Second Team center for 1950-51. Doug Bentley was chosen as the First Team left winger in 1942-43, 1943-44 and 1946-47. He was the Second Team center in 1948-49. Alex Delvecchio was selected as Second Team center in 1952-53. He also made the Second Team as a left winger in 1958-59. Messier was selected as a left winger on the First Team in 1981-82 and 1982-83, as well as a Second Team left winger in 1983-84. He was later selected to the First All-Star Team as a center in 1989-90 and 1991-92.

Names and Numbers

The identification of a player by a name or number brings immediate significance to it. If the names Esposito or Orr are mentioned, a flood of details cross your mind. The number 9 brings instant recognition of several players: Richard, Howe and Hull. What about number 99 or number 66? The connections between these numbers and Gretzky and Lemieux are unmistakable. In hockey, the association between names and numbers carries on even further, linking players with their statistics and teammates. Names and numbers have great importance.

FIRST PERIOD - NUMBER GAMES

1. What number did Hall of Fame defenseman Babe Siebert wear during his three seasons with the Montreal Canadiens?

Babe Siebert was traded from Boston to Montreal in September of 1936. He wore sweater number 1 while he played defense for the Montreal Canadiens in his final three NHL seasons. Siebert was a standout on the Canadiens' defense, winning the Hart Trophy in 1936-37 and being selected to the First All-Star Team in 1936-37 and 1937-38. He died in a drowning accident in August of 1939.

2. Which NHL franchise will be the first to retire ten sweater numbers?

The Boston Bruins will retire their tenth sweater number when Cam Neely's number 8 is honored during the 2003-04 season. Previously retired numbers by the Bruins recognize Eddie Shore (2), Lionel Hitchman (3), Bobby Orr (4), Dit Clapper (5), Phil Esposito (7), Johnny Bucyk (9), Milt Schmidt (15), Terry O'Reilly (24) and Ray Bourque (77).

3. Name the two individuals who were awarded the Conn Smythe Trophy while sporting the number 27.

Reggie Leach of the Philadelphia Flyers wore number 27 when he received the Conn Smythe Trophy for his nineteen-goal performance in the 1976 Stanley Cup playoffs. Goaltender Ron Hextall of the Philadelphia Flyers was also wearing number 27 when he was presented with the Conn Smythe Trophy for his efforts in the 1987 playoffs.

4. Name the three future Hall of Famers who all wore number 4 while playing defense for the Detroit Red Wings at some point during the 1960s.

Red Kelly sported number 4 in 1960, until he was traded in February of that year. Bill Gadsby wore it as a member of the Red Wings from 1961-62 until 1965-66. Leo Boivin had sweater number 4 in 1966-67, his only full season with the Red Wings.

5. Who was the first player to score a goal for the Montreal Canadiens while wearing sweater number 29?

Jean Chabot scored eighteen times while wearing number 29 for the Montreal Canadiens in 1983-84. The number had previously been worn by seven different goalies, most notably Ken Dryden, between 1971 and 1979. Goaltenders Rick Wamsley and Mark Holden, along with skaters Dave Orleski and John Newberry, wore sweater number 29 at some point in the four seasons between 1980 and 1983. However, Orleski and Newberry were both unable to record a goal as Canadiens.

6. What are the four highest sweater numbers to be worn by winners of the Hart Trophy?

The four highest sweater numbers to be worn by winners of the Hart Trophy are: number 68 (Jaromir Jagr), number 88 (Eric Lindros), number 91 (Sergei Fedorov) and number 99 (Wayne Gretzky). Gretzky captured the award a total of nine times in the 1980s. Fedorov, Lindros and Jagr were all presented with the Hart during the 1990s.

7. What four sweater numbers did Howie Morenz wear in his NHL career?

Morenz wore sweater numbers 3, 6, 7 and 11 at various times throughout his NHL career. Morenz broke into the league with the Montreal Canadiens in 1923-24 and wore what would become his famous sweater number 7 for those first two seasons. For the 1925-26 season, Morenz switched from sweater number 7 to sweater number 6 when his teammate, Odie Cleghorn, moved on to the Pittsburgh Pirates. It is not clear why Morenz was assigned number 6 rather than number 7 for the 1925-26 season, but unhappy with his play, Morenz suggested that he would like to return to his familiar number 7 for the following year. Morenz wore number 7 for the next eight seasons as a member of the Montreal Canadiens before being dealt to Chicago in 1934. As a Black Hawk, Morenz sported number 3. He was dealt to the New York Rangers in January of 1936. Here he donned number 11 for the remainder of the season. Morenz returned to Montreal for his final NHL season of 1936-37, where he again wore number 7. Following a career-ending injury, he tragically died in March, 1937. Number 7 was retired by the Montreal Canadiens to honor the contribution of Howie Morenz to the franchise.

8. What is the only sweater number to be retired by the Ottawa Senators?

The Ottawa Senators have retired number 8 to recognize Frank Finnigan. He played for the original Senators' NHL franchise in ten of the eleven seasons between 1923-24 and 1933-34. Finnigan was also a major supporter of Ottawa's successful bid to re-enter the league with a new franchise for the 1992-93 season.

9. Name the last three players to have worn number 9 as a member of the Detroit Red Wings.
(Hint: They all became Hall of Famers.)

Obviously, Gordie Howe was the last to wear this sweater number, taking it up in his second NHL season of 1947-48 and wearing it through to his retirement in 1970-71. The Red Wings retired sweater number 9 to honor Howe on March 12, 1972. Number 9 was also worn by two other future Hall of Famers in the two seasons preceding 1947-48. Sid Abel had returned from military service in the 1945-46 season to find Joe Carveth wearing Abel's familiar number 12. Abel donned number 9 for the ten games he played for the Red Wings in 1945-46. Carveth was traded to Boston for Roy Conacher in August of 1946, which allowed Abel to once again take up his familiar number 12. Conacher then took over number 9 which had been worn by Abel. Conacher had worn number 9 with the Bruins before coming to Detroit. Gordie Howe, who was a rookie on this 1946-47 team, wore number 17. When Conacher was traded to the Chicago Black Hawks for the 1947-48 season, Howe switched from number 17 to number 9. Lower sweater numbers were preferred by players in those days because it gave them a lower berth on the overnight train trips.

10. Name the five forwards wearing number 10 in the Northwest Division at the close of the 2002-03 NHL season.

Player	Team
Serge Aubin	Colorado
Dave Lowry	Calgary
Shawn Horcoff	Edmonton
Marian Gaborik	Minnesota
Trevor Letowski	Vancouver

11. How many times has the Norris Trophy been won by a defenseman wearing a double-digit sweater number?

There have been twelve times over the first fifty Norris Trophy presentations where the winner wore a double-digit sweater number.

Player	Norris Trophy	Team	Number
Tom Johnson	1958-59	Montreal Canadiens	10
Larry Robinson	1976-77, 1979-80	Montreal Canadiens	19
Randy Carlyle	1980-81	Pittsburgh Penguins	25
Doug Wilson	1981-82	Chicago Black Hawks	24
Ray Bourque	1987-88, 1989-90, 1990-91, 1993-94	Boston Bruins	77
Chris Chelios	1988-89	Montreal Canadiens	24
Paul Coffey	1994-95	Detroit Red Wings	77
Chris Pronger	1999-2000	St. Louis Blues	44

12. Name the only three players to have worn sweater number 22 with the Montreal Canadiens between 1955-56 and 1983-84.

Only Don Marshall, John Ferguson and Steve Shutt wore number 22 for the Canadiens through these twenty-nine seasons. Marshall was one of three players to sport sweater number 22 with the team in 1954-55, but became the only player to wear it in 1955-56. This remained his number until he was traded to the Rangers in June of 1963. Ferguson wore number 22 throughout his entire career with the Montreal Canadiens from 1963-64 through 1970-71. No one wore the number in the 1971-72 season with the Canadiens. Steve Shutt put it on in 1972-73, wearing it until he was dealt to the Los Angeles Kings, ten games into the 1984-85 season.

13. Name the only two individuals who have worn number 13 as members of the Quebec Nordiques in the NHL.

Mats Sundin was the first, wearing number 13 from his rookie season in 1990-91 until his trade to Toronto in 1994. In 1995, which was the last year that the Nordiques played in Quebec, Valeri Kamensky wore number 13. Kamensky continued to sport number 13 as a member of the Colorado Avalanche, until moving to the Rangers in 1999. Dan Hinote is the only player to have skated with this number on the Avalanche since Kamensky's departure.

14. Name the first two players to wear sweater number 4 with the Montreal Canadiens in the NHL.

Newsy Lalonde wore sweater number 4 during the first five seasons that the Montreal Canadiens were in the National Hockey League, from 1917-18 through 1921-22. The Canadiens traded Lalonde to Saskatoon of the Western Canadian Hockey League in September of 1922, in return for Aurel Joliat. Joliat took over Lalonde's sweater number 4 and wore it through his sixteen seasons with the Montreal Canadiens until his retirement in 1938. It is surprising that this number was not retired at that point, considering the major contributions these two Hall of Famers made to the Canadiens. Sixteen other players wore this sweater number between 1938 and 1953, when the legendary Jean Beliveau claimed it. Number 4 was retired to recognize Jean Beliveau's contribution to the Canadiens.

15. Who wore sweater number 9 for Team Canada in the 1972 Summit Series?

Bill Goldsworthy of the Minnesota North Stars wore sweater number 9 in the 1972 Summit Series. Goldsworthy participated in three games, recording a goal and an assist. Bobby Hull, who no doubt would have sported the number had he played, had recently signed a contract with the Winnipeg Jets of the WHA and was ineligible to participate.

16. When defenseman Dave Manson was traded to the Montreal Canadiens in 1997, he became the eighth player to wear number 37 for the team. The previous seven individuals had all been goalies. How many of them can you name?

Goalie	Seasons Wearing 37
Steve Penney	1983-84 to 1985-86
Randy Exelby	1988-89
Jean-Claude Bergeron	1990-91
Andre Racicot	1992-93 to 1993-94
Martin Brochu	1994-95 (did not play)
Jose Theodore	1995-96
Tomas Vokoun	1996-97

17. This player wore number 27 with the Quebec Nordiques in the 1979-80 season. He scored two goals and racked up 74 penalty minutes. He later went on to become an NHL referee.

Paul Stewart played three partial seasons in the WHA with the Edmonton Oilers and the Cincinnati Stingers, before being claimed by the Quebec Nordiques in the WHA Dispersal Draft. His short playing career in the NHL was followed by a few stints in the minor leagues, before re-entering the league as a referee in March of 1987. Stewart retired from refereeing following the 2002-03 NHL season.

18. What were the four highest sweater numbers worn by goaltenders in the 2002-03 NHL season?

Sweater numbers 50, 60, 70 and 80 were the four highest to be worn by goaltenders during the 2002-03 season. Reinhard Divis sported number 50 for the St. Louis Blues in his two NHL appearances of the season.

Montreal Canadien Jose Theodore wore number 60. Tim Thomas was number 70 in four appearances with the Boston Bruins and Kevin Weekes had number 80 as a Carolina Hurricane.

19. Name the first four sweater numbers that were retired by the Edmonton Oilers.

The most recent sweater number to be retired by the Oilers was 31, which was honored in recognition of Grant Fuhr in October of 2003. Fuhr was inducted into the Hockey Hall of Fame in November of the same year. The three previous sweater numbers retired by the Edmonton Oilers were: number 3 (Al Hamilton), number 17 (Jari Kurri) and, of course, number 99 (Wayne Gretzky).

20. Who was the last player to wear number 20 for the Toronto Maple Leafs before Ed Belfour?

Jeff Farkas wore sweater number 20 in six regular season and two playoff games in the 2001-02 NHL season. The last Toronto player to wear the number on a regular basis was Mike Johnson. He wore number 20 as a Leaf from 1996-97 until his trade to the Tampa Bay Lightning during the 1999-2000 season.

SECOND PERIOD - HOW MANY?

1. How many teams won a playoff series in four games in the 2003 Stanley Cup playoffs?

The Anaheim Mighty Ducks were the only team able to achieve a sweep in the 2003 playoffs, which they did on two occasions. They took the Detroit Red Wings in four straight games during the Western Conference quarter-final. They then swept the Minnesota Wild in the Western Conference final.

2. How many NHL franchises have won at least five Stanley Cups between 1918 and 2003?

There are five NHL franchises that have won five or more Stanley Cups in the years between 1918 and 2003.

Stanley Cup Championships 1918 to 2003

Team	Cup Wins
Montreal Canadiens	23
Toronto Arenas/St. Pats/Maple Leafs	13
Detroit Red Wings	10
Boston Bruins	5
Edmonton Oilers	5

3. How many players recorded over two hundred minutes in penalties in the 2002-03 NHL season?

There were three players with over 200 penalty minutes in 2002-03. Jody Shelley of the Columbus Blue Jackets was the penalty minute leader with 249 minutes. He was followed by Reed Low of the St. Louis Blues who was assigned 234 minutes and Matt Johnson of the Minnesota Wild who recorded 201. Wade Belak of Toronto, Peter Worrell of Florida and Barret Jackman of St. Louis, all came close as they each recorded 190 minutes or more in penalties in this same season.

4. How many individuals have played on five Stanley Cup winners with the Toronto Maple Leafs?

Walter "Turk" Broda, Don Metz and Ted Kennedy are the only three players to have skated with five Stanley Cup winners as Maple Leafs. However, numerous players have their names on the Cup four times as a Maple Leaf. Goaltender Turk Broda's first Cup victory was in 1942 followed by 1947, 1948, 1949 and 1951. Broda missed the 1945 Stanley Cup victory when he was serving overseas in the Canadian Army. Don Metz won the Cup in 1942, 1945, 1947, 1948, and 1949. Ted Kennedy helped to capture the Stanley Cup in 1945, 1947, 1948, 1949 and 1951.

5. How many times has the Art Ross Trophy gone to a player(s) from the same team for seven consecutive seasons?

Three teams have had seven consecutive winners of the Art Ross Trophy. The Boston Bruins' Phil Esposito won it five times, while Bobby Orr won it twice between 1968-69 and 1974-75. Wayne Gretzky of the Edmonton Oilers was the recipient seven seasons in a row from 1980-81 to 1986-87. Jaromir Jagr and Mario Lemieux of the Pittsburgh Penguins took the Art Ross for a streak of seven seasons between them from 1994-95 to 2000-01. Jagr won the trophy on five occasions, while Lemieux had the honor twice.

6. How many teams played overtime in the 2003 Stanley Cup playoffs?

Thirteen teams played overtime in the 2003 playoffs. Boston, Edmonton and St. Louis were the only playoff teams not to see any overtime action.

7. How many times in the past twenty-three NHL seasons have all of the top ten scoring leaders been Canadian-born?

In the twenty-three seasons between 1980-81 and 2002-03, this has only happened once, in 1990-91.

Scoring Leaders in the 1990-91 NHL Season

Player	Team	Points	Birthplace
Wayne Gretzky	Los Angeles	163	Brantford, ON
Brett Hull	St. Louis	131	Belleville, ON
Adam Oates	St. Louis	115	Weston, ON
Mark Recchi	Pittsburgh	113	Kamloops, BC
John Cullen	Pittsburgh/Hartford	110	Puslinch, ON
Joe Sakic	Quebec	109	Burnaby, BC
Steve Yzerman	Detroit	108	Cranbrook, BC
Theoren Fleury	Calgary	104	Oxbow, SASK
Al MacInnis	Calgary	103	Inverness, NS
Steve Larmer	Chicago	101	Peterborough, ON

8. How many players have won the Hart Trophy at least four times?

There have been three individuals win four or more Hart awards. The first to do this was Eddie Shore. This outstanding Boston defenseman was presented the Hart Trophy four times in six years. His first win was in 1932-33 and he received the trophy for a final time in 1937-38. Gordie Howe was awarded the Hart Trophy a total of six times as a Red Wing, between 1951-52 and 1962-63. Wayne Gretzky of the Edmonton Oilers won the trophy for eight consecutive seasons, 1979-80 through 1986-87. He also received the honor for a ninth time in 1988-89 as a member of the Los Angeles Kings.

9. How many times has the home team won every game in a seven game Stanley Cup final series?

This has happened on three occasions.

Year	Cup Winner	Finalists
1955	Detroit Red Wings	Montreal Canadiens
1965	Montreal Canadiens	Chicago Black Hawks
2003	New Jersey Devils	Anaheim Mighty Ducks

10. How many individuals have played on Stanley Cup winners with three different NHL franchises?

Joe Nieuwendyk of the 2002-03 New Jersey Devils became the sixth player to win the Stanley Cup with three different NHL franchises. Nieuwendyk's previous Cup victories were with the Calgary Flames in 1989 and the Dallas Stars in 1999. The five previous individuals to be Cup winners with three different NHL franchises were: Gord Pettinger, Al Arbour, Larry Hillman, Claude Lemieux and Mike Keane.

11. How many overtime games did Anaheim win in the 2003 Stanley Cup playoffs?

The Anaheim Mighty Ducks had a 7-0 record in overtime in the 2003 Stanley Cup playoffs. They defeated Detroit twice in overtime in the Western Conference quarter-final; Dallas twice in the Western Conference semi-final; Minnesota on one occasion in the Western Conference final; and the New Jersey Devils in games three and four of the Stanley Cup final.

12. Seven players saw action with three different NHL teams in the 2002-03 season. How many can you name?

Player	2002-03 NHL Teams
Harold Druken	Vancouver, Toronto, Carolina
Josh Green	Edmonton, New York Rangers, Washington
Tomi Kallio	Atlanta, Columbus, Philadelphia
Dan McGillis	Philadelphia, San Jose, Boston
Jonathan Sim	Dallas, Nashville, Los Angeles
Todd Warriner	Vancouver, Philadelphia, Nashville
Dmitry Yushkevich	Florida, Los Angeles, Philadelphia

13. How many cities played host to an NHL All-Star game over the twenty-two matches from 1947 to 1969?

Only four cities hosted the annual All-Star game from its inception in 1947 until 1969. The game was played in Montreal nine times, while Toronto was the site for seven matches. Detroit hosted the All-Stars on four occasions and Chicago held the event twice.

14. How many times has an NHL team been in the Stanley Cup final in five or more consecutive years?

This has happened on three occasions. The Montreal Canadiens reached the final for ten consecutive seasons from 1951 to 1960. The Canadiens again appeared in the final playoff series in a five-year streak between 1965 and 1969. The New York Islanders were in the final for five consecutive years from 1980 to 1984.

15. How many games went into at least a second overtime period in the 2003 Stanley Cup playoffs?

A record nine games went into at least a second overtime period in the 2003 playoffs.

Multiple Period Overtime Games in 2003 Playoffs

Date	Result	Game-Winning Goal
April 10	Anaheim 2 at Detroit 1 (3 OT)	Paul Kariya
April 14	Ottawa 3 at New York Islanders 2 (2 OT)	Todd White
April 14	Philadelphia 3 at Toronto 4 (2 OT)	Tomas Kaberle
April 16	Philadelphia 3 at Toronto 2 (3 OT)	Mark Recchi
April 20	Tampa Bay 2 at Washington 1 (3 OT)	Martin St. Louis
April 21	Philadelphia 1 at Toronto 2 (2 OT)	Travis Green
April 24	Anaheim 4 at Dallas 3 (5 OT)	Petr Sykora
May 2	Tampa Bay 1 at New Jersey 2 (3 OT)	Grant Marshall
May 10	Anaheim 1 at Minnesota 0 (2 OT)	Petr Sykora

16. How many times have brothers on NHL teams faced each other in the Stanley Cup final?

This has happened on five occasions. George Boucher of the Ottawa Senators faced brother Billy with the Boston Bruins in 1927, which was the first time two NHL teams had met in a Stanley Cup final. Paul

Thompson of the New York Rangers and his brother, goaltender Cecil "Tiny" Thompson of the Bruins, took part in the 1929 final. In 1935, brothers Charlie Conacher of the Toronto Maple Leafs and Lionel Conacher of the Montreal Maroons met in a final series. Kenny Reardon of the Montreal Canadiens and brother Terry of the Boston Bruins skated on opposite sides in 1946. Scott Niedermayer of the New Jersey Devils and brother Rob of the Anaheim Mighty Ducks met in the 2003 Stanley Cup final.

17. For how many seasons was the NHL a six team league?

The NHL was composed of six teams for twenty-six seasons. The Original Six, as it was known, existed for twenty-five seasons from 1942-43 to 1966-67. There was also one other season when there were six teams in the NHL. In 1924-25, the league had expanded by two, with the Montreal Maroons and the Boston Bruins joining the Hamilton Tigers, the Toronto St. Pats, the Montreal Canadiens and the Ottawa Senators. The league expanded to seven teams in 1925-26, increased to ten in 1926-27, before it dropped back to six by 1942-43.

18. How many individuals have won the Hart Trophy as a member of a last place team?

The only two individuals on a last place team to have been awarded the Hart Trophy were Tom "Cowboy" Anderson of the 1941-42 Brooklyn Americans and goaltender Al Rollins of the 1953-54 Chicago Black Hawks.

19. How many Canadian franchises have won the Presidents' Trophy?

The Calgary Flames, the Edmonton Oilers and the Ottawa Senators are the only three Canadian NHL franchises to have won the Presidents' Trophy. The award is presented to the club with the best overall record in the NHL regular season. The Edmonton Oilers were awarded the trophy in the first two seasons of its presentation, 1985-86 and 1986-87, followed by the Calgary Flames who won it the next two years. Most recently, the Presidents' Trophy was presented to the 2002-03 Ottawa Senators.

20. How many times have the Toronto Maple Leafs finished last overall in the National Hockey League?

The Toronto franchise has only finished last overall on two occasions as the Maple Leafs. The first time, the Leafs ended in sixth place in 1957-58. The only other occasion was a 48 point finish, placing them fifth in the Norris Division and last overall in the 1984-85 season. The Toronto Arenas also finished last overall among the three teams competing in the 1918-19 NHL season, but actually discontinued play in February because of their disastrous showing.

THIRD PERIOD
WHAT'S THE CONNECTION?

1. Dave Andreychuk, Phil Housley, Scott Mellanby, Adam Oates, James Patrick, Steve Thomas

At the end of the 2002-03 season, these were the six individuals still playing in the NHL who have played the most NHL games without ever winning a Stanley Cup.

Player	Regular Season	Playoff	Total
Dave Andreychuk	1515	139	1654
Phil Housley	1495	85	1580
Adam Oates	1277	163	1440
Steve Thomas	1191	168	1359
Scott Mellanby	1223	128	1351
James Patrick	1225	117	1342

2. Rick Bowness, Butch Goring, Lorne Henning, Peter Laviolette, Bill Stewart, Steve Stirling

These are the six head coaches that Mike Milbury has had behind the bench with the New York Islanders since he took over as general manager in December of 1995. Milbury has also stepped in as head coach for the Islanders himself during this time.

3. Ed Belfour, Fred Brathwaite, Curtis Joseph, Dwayne Roloson

None of these goaltenders were ever selected by an NHL team in the Entry Draft. All began their careers signing on as free agents. Fred Brathwaite signed as a free agent with Edmonton in 1993. He had played in the Ontario Hockey League with London, Detroit and Oshawa. Belfour was a free agent in September of 1987, when he signed with Chicago. He was in net in the 1986-87 season with the University of North Dakota. Curtis Joseph signed with St. Louis in June of 1989. Joseph had played with the University of Wisconsin team in 1988-89. Dwayne Roloson had tended net in four seasons at the University of Massachusetts/Lowell, when he was signed as a free agent by Calgary in July of 1994.

4. Tyler Arnason, Jay Bouwmeester, Sebastian Caron, Barret Jackman, Rick Nash, Henrik Zetterberg

This is the rookie All-Star Team for the 2002-03 NHL season.

Player	Team	Position
Sebastian Caron	Pittsburgh Penguins	goalie
Jay Bouwmeester	Florida Panthers	defense
Barret Jackman	St. Louis Blues	defense
Tyler Arnason	Chicago Blackhawks	forward
Rick Nash	Columbus Blue Jackets	forward
Henrik Zetterberg	Detroit Red Wings	forward

5. Real Cloutier, Tony McKegney, Brent Ashton, Doug Shedden, Marc Fortier, Mike Ricci

These are the only six players to have worn sweater number 9 in the sixteen NHL seasons of the Quebec Nordiques.

6. Ed Belfour, Lorne Chabot, Tony Esposito, Charlie Gardiner, Glenn Hall

These are the only five goaltenders to have been selected to an NHL First All-Star Team as members of the Chicago Blackhawks. Gardiner was selected as First All-Star goalie in three seasons: 1930-31, 1931-32 and 1933-34. Chabot made First All-Star in 1934-35. Glenn Hall had the honor of being First All-Star goaltender as a member of the Black Hawks on five separate occasions, between 1957-58 and 1965-66. Tony Esposito was the goalie selected three times between 1969-70 and 1979-80, while Ed Belfour was chosen as a Blackhawk in 1990-91, and again in 1992-93.

7. Frank Boucher, Bill Carson, Corb Denneny, Pete Kelly, Mush March, Howie Morenz

These are the first players to score a Stanley Cup-winning goal for each of the Original Six NHL franchises.

Year	Stanley Cup Champion	Winning Goal Scorer
1918	Toronto Arenas	Corb Denneny
1924	Montreal Canadiens	Howie Morenz
1928	New York Rangers	Frank Boucher
1929	Boston Bruins	Bill Carson
1934	Chicago Black Hawks	Harold "Mush" March
1936	Detroit Red Wings	Pete Kelly

8. Doug Jarvis, Steve Larmer, Craig Ramsay, Garry Unger

These are the four individuals who have played in the longest consecutive game streaks in NHL history. Doug Jarvis holds the record appearing in 964 consecutive games with the Montreal Canadiens, the Washington Capitals and the Hartford Whalers, from the beginning of the 1975-76 season to early in 1987-88. Garry Unger skated in 914 consecutive games between 1968 and 1979 while playing for Toronto, Detroit, St. Louis and finally, the Atlanta Flames. Steve Larmer appeared in 884 consecutive games with the Chicago Blackhawks from 1982-83 to 1992-93. Buffalo Sabre Craig Ramsay appeared in 776 consecutive regular season games, from late in the 1972-73 season through to February of 1983.

9. Mel Bridgman, Barry Dean, Ralph Klassen, Brian Maxwell, Rick Lapointe

These were the top five selections in the 1975 Amateur Draft.

1975 Amateur Draft

Selection	Player	Selected By	Selected From
1	Mel Bridgman	Philadelphia Flyers*	Victoria Cougars
2	Barry Dean	Kansas City Scouts	Medicine Hat Tigers
3	Ralph Klassen	California Golden Seals	Saskatoon Blades
4	Bryan Maxwell	Minnesota North Stars	Medicine Hat Tigers
5	Rick Lapointe	Detroit Red Wings	Victoria Cougars

*The Philadelphia Flyers had obtained the first pick overall from the Washington Capitals in a trade.

10. Sergei Fedorov, Tomas Holmstrom, Luc Robitaille, Brendan Shanahan, Jason Woolley, Henrik Zetterberg

These are the six scorers for the Detroit Red Wings in the 2003 Stanley Cup playoffs. Detroit was only able to put six goals past Jean-Sebastian Giguere in Anaheim's net as they were swept by the Mighty Ducks in four games in the Conference quarter-final.

11. Tom Barrasso, Ed Belfour, Pavel Bure, Bryan Berard, Chris Drury, Joe Nieuwendyk, Luc Robitaille, Teemu Selanne

All of these individuals are former winners of the Calder Trophy. Their 2002-03 teams were different than the teams they played on during their Calder-winning season.

Player	Calder Trophy Season	2002-03 Team
Chris Drury	1998-99, Colorado Avalanche	Calgary Flames
Bryan Berard	1996-97, New York Islanders	Boston Bruins
Teemu Selanne	1992-93, Winnipeg Jets	San Jose Sharks
Pavel Bure	1991-92, Vancouver Canucks	New York Rangers
Ed Belfour	1990-91, Chicago Blackhawks	Toronto Maple Leafs
Joe Nieuwendyk	1987-88, Calgary Flames	New Jersey Devils
Luc Robitaille	1986-87, Los Angeles Kings	Detroit Red Wings
Tom Barrasso	1983-84, Buffalo Sabres	St. Louis Blues

12. Dale Hunter, Claude Lemieux, Chris Nilan

This group of individuals are the career leaders in penalty minutes in the NHL playoffs. Dale Hunter retired as the leader having accumulated 729 minutes with Quebec, Washington and Colorado over 186 games in eighteen playoff years. Chris Nilan recorded 541 penalty minutes in 111 games in twelve playoff years with the Montreal Canadiens, the New York Rangers and the Boston Bruins. Claude Lemieux has served 529 playoff penalty minutes while playing with Montreal, New Jersey, Colorado, Phoenix and Dallas. He has appeared in 233 games over his first seventeen playoff years in the league.

13. Marian Hossa, Jarome Iginla, Saku Koivu, Alex Mogilny, Markus Naslund, Ryan Smyth

These were the leading scorers for each of the six Canadian NHL franchises in 2002-03.

Leading Scorers of Canadian NHL Franchises 2002-03

Player	Team	GP	G	A	PTS
Markus Naslund	Vancouver Canucks	82	48	56	104
Marian Hossa	Ottawa Senators	80	45	35	80
Alex Mogilny	Toronto Maple Leafs	73	33	46	79
Saku Koivu	Montreal Canadiens	82	21	50	71
Jarome Iginla	Calgary Flames	75	35	32	67
Ryan Smyth	Edmonton Oilers	66	27	34	61

14. King Clancy, Hap Day, Red Horner

All three of these Hall of Famers and members of the 1932 Stanley Cup-winning Toronto Maple Leafs went on to officiate as referees or linesmen in the National Hockey League.

15. Ray Bourque, Gordie Howe, Larry Murphy, Larry Robinson, Scott Stevens

These are the only five individuals to have played in the NHL playoffs in twenty different seasons as of the end of 2003. Bourque made an appearance in twenty-one playoffs, while Stevens matched the mark of Howe, Murphy and Robinson, skating in his twentieth playoffs in 2003.

16. Glenn Anderson, Red Kelly, Kevin Lowe, Mark Messier, Bryan Trottier

All of these NHL players won the Stanley Cup at least six times. None of them, however, were Cup champions as members of the Montreal Canadiens.

Player	Stanley Cup Teams and Years
Red Kelly	Detroit (1950, 1952, 1954, 1955)
	Toronto (1962, 1963, 1964, 1967)
Bryan Trottier	Islanders (1980, 1981, 1982, 1983)
	Pittsburgh (1991, 1992)
Glenn Anderson	Edmonton (1984, 1985, 1987, 1988, 1990)
	Rangers (1994)
Kevin Lowe	Edmonton (1984, 1985, 1987, 1988, 1990)
	Rangers (1994)
Mark Messier	Edmonton (1984, 1985, 1987, 1988, 1990)
	Rangers (1994)

17. Ron Chipperfield, Rick Ley, Lars-Erik Sjoberg, Marc Tardif

Rick Ley (Hartford Whalers), Ron Chipperfield (Edmonton Oilers), Lars-Erik Sjoberg (Winnipeg Jets) and Mark Tardif (Quebec Nordiques) were the first captains of the four expansion franchises that entered the NHL as survivors of the WHA in 1979.

18. Dave Andreychuk, Bill Gadsby, Phil Housley, Harry Howell, Doug Mohns, James Patrick, Dean Prentice, Jean Ratelle, Norm Ullman, John Vanbiesbrouck

These individuals have played in at least twenty NHL seasons and have never been on a Stanley Cup winner to the end of the 2002-03 season.

19. Sid Abel, Syl Apps, Doug Bentley, Toe Blake, Dit Clapper, Ott Heller

These six players were the captains of the NHL teams in 1942-43, the first season of what became known as the Original Six years.

Original Six Captains 1942-43

Boston Bruins	Dit Clapper
Chicago Black Hawks	Doug Bentley
Detroit Red Wings	Sid Abel
Montreal Canadiens	Toe Blake
New York Rangers	Ott Heller
Toronto Maple Leafs	Syl Apps

20. Dave Balon, Bob Baun, Earl Ingarfield, Gord Labossiere, Jim Roberts, Ed Van Impe

In the NHL Expansion Draft in 1967, these were the first players, aside from goalies, selected by the six new teams.

Player	Selected By	Selected From
Dave Balon	Minnesota North Stars	Montreal Canadiens
Bob Baun	California Seals	Toronto Maple Leafs
Earl Ingarfield	Pittsburgh Penguins	New York Rangers
Gord Labossiere	Los Angeles Kings	Montreal Canadiens
Jim Roberts	St. Louis Blues	Montreal Canadiens
Ed Van Impe	Philadelphia Flyers	Chicago Black Hawks

Peter Forsberg was awarded the Art Ross Trophy and the Hart Trophy for the 2002-03 season.

PHOTO REPLAY

1. Who was the last player, prior to Peter Forsberg, to win both the Art Ross and the Hart in the same season?

Jaromir Jagr of the Pittsburgh Penguins took both trophies in the 1998-99 season.

2. Who was the last player to win the Art Ross Trophy wearing sweater number 21, prior to Peter Forsberg?

Stan Mikita wore number 21 for the Chicago Black Hawks. He was awarded the Art Ross Trophy in four of the five seasons between 1963-64 and 1967-68.

3. Name the two players, other than Peter Forsberg, who skated with the Quebec Nordiques and were still members of the Colorado Avalanche in 2002-03.

Peter Forsberg won the Calder Trophy as the NHL's top rookie with the Quebec Nordiques in 1995. Adam Foote and Joe Sakic were also playing with this NHL franchise that year, prior to the team moving to Colorado. They were the only three players from the 1995 Nordiques remaining with the Avalanche in 2002-03.

4. Name the only Swedish-born winner of the Calder Trophy, other than Peter Forsberg.

Daniel Alfredsson of the Ottawa Senators was awarded the Calder Trophy in 1995-96, the season following Forsberg's outstanding rookie year in Quebec.

Moving On

From the time players enter the National Hockey League through the Entry Draft, they must live with trade rumors surfacing and unsettling their lives. Free agency is also responsible for frequent location changes. Fans analyze the shifting league, taking their turn at playing general manager. The days and hours leading up to the trading deadline are much anticipated. Trades are part of the game. However, the privilege of playing hockey overrides the inconsistency in lifestyle. The love of the game usually wins.

FIRST PERIOD - WHO AM I?

1. I scored five goals against my former team in the 2003 Stanley Cup final.

Jeff Friesen recorded five of his ten playoff goals against the Anaheim Mighty Ducks in the Stanley Cup final. Friesen had been traded to the Devils, along with Oleg Tverdovsky and Maxim Balmochnykh, in return for Petr Sykora, Mike Commodore, Jean-Francois Damphousse and Igor Pohanka. This trade took place on July 6, 2002.

2. I accompanied Brad Park and Jean Ratelle in a blockbuster trade to the Boston Bruins in November of 1975.

Joe Zanussi was traded along with Brad Park and Jean Ratelle to the Boston Bruins from the New York Rangers for Phil Esposito and Carol Vadnais on November 7, 1975. Zanussi went on to play sixty regular season and four playoff games for the Boston Bruins that season. Zanussi saw action in only twenty-seven other NHL games.

3. I was traded by Philadelphia to Montreal in 1995, then returned to Philadelphia from Montreal in another trade in 1999.

Mark Recchi was sent to Montreal, along with a draft pick, in exchange for John LeClair, Eric Desjardins and Gilbert Dionne on February 9, 1995. After seeing plenty of ice time in five seasons with the Montreal Canadiens, Recchi returned to Philadelphia in a trade for Danius Zubrus and two draft choices on March 10, 1999.

4. I am the only goaltender who was traded during a Vezina Trophy-winning season.

Michel "Bunny" Larocque won the 1980-81 Vezina with Montreal goaltenders Denis Herron and Richard Sevigny. At that time, the Vezina Trophy was awarded to the goaltenders of the team with the best goals-against average for the season. Although Herron and Sevigny remained with the team, Larocque was dealt to Toronto in March of 1981, marking the only time that a goaltender was traded during his Vezina Trophy-winning season.

5. I racked up my second highest penalty minute total of 405 minutes in a single NHL season while playing on both the Los Angeles Kings and the Pittsburgh Penguins.

Dave Schultz and penalties are synonymous with the Philadelphia Flyers, especially considering his record 472 minutes in the 1974-75 season. Schultz recorded his second highest total ever while splitting a season between the Kings and the Penguins. Schultz had been dealt to the Los Angeles Kings prior to the 1976-77 season. In the first eight games of the next season, 1977-78, he already had accumulated 27 minutes in penalties. He was then dealt to Pittsburgh, where he went on to receive 378 minutes in 66 games, for a total of 405 minutes in 1977-78.

6. I tended net for my eighth NHL franchise in 2002-03.

Ron Tugnutt has played goal for eight different NHL franchises in his career. He was drafted by the Quebec Nordiques in the 1986 Entry Draft and saw action with them in five different seasons, before being traded to Edmonton in March of 1992. Tugnutt has also been in net for Anaheim, Montreal, Ottawa, Pittsburgh, Columbus and, most recently, Dallas with the Stars.

7. I am the only player ever obtained in a trade involving Tim Horton.

Denis Dupere was sent from the New York Rangers to Toronto in May of 1970 to complete a trade that saw Tim Horton move from the Maple Leafs to the Rangers two months earlier. Horton later went on to both Pittsburgh and Buffalo via the Intra-League Draft. Dupere played in four seasons with the Maple Leafs and in four additional NHL seasons between Washington, St. Louis, Kansas City and the Colorado Rockies.

8. I was claimed by the Kansas City Scouts from the Stanley Cup champion Philadelphia Flyers in the NHL Expansion Draft in 1974.

Simon Nolet was claimed by the Kansas City Scouts in the 1974 Expansion Draft. While Nolet had been a solid performer with the Flyers during their first seven NHL seasons, he had his best individual season in 1974-75 with the Kansas City Scouts when he recorded twenty-six goals and fifty-eight points. Nolet also served as the captain of the Kansas City Scouts/Colorado Rockies for most of the first three seasons of the franchise.

9. I was obtained by the Chicago Blackhawks in exchange for Brian Noonan and Stephane Matteau in March of 1994.

The Chicago Blackhawks obtained Tony Amonte at the trade deadline in 1994. Matteau and Noonan went on to win the Cup with the Rangers that spring. Amonte recorded more than thirty goals for the Blackhawks in six consecutive seasons between 1995-96 and 2000-01. Amonte signed on as a free agent with Phoenix in July of 2002. At the close of the 2002-03 season, he was with the Philadelphia Flyers.

10. I am the only goaltender to be included in a trade involving Phil Esposito.

Jack Norris was traded from the Boston Bruins, along with Gilles Marotte and Pit Martin, in a deal with the Chicago Black Hawks in return for Phil Esposito, Ken Hodge and Fred Stanfield on May 15, 1967. The trade is often sighted as one of the most lop-sided trades in NHL history. Norris had been in net in twenty-three games with the Boston Bruins in 1964-65. He went on to play in a mere ten games over 1967-68 and 1968-69 with the Chicago Black Hawks, before finishing his career as a Los Angeles King in 1970-71, seeing action in only twenty-five games that season.

11. I was traded to the Detroit Red Wings by the Toronto Maple Leafs in return for Red Kelly.

The Toronto Maple Leafs traded Marc Reaume to the Detroit Red Wings in exchange for Leonard "Red" Kelly on February 10, 1960. Kelly had vetoed an earlier trade, opting to retire rather than report to the New York Rangers. Kelly's threat to retire prompted the Red Wings to take Reaume from the Maple Leafs, ensuring a trade to a team which Kelly found acceptable.

12. I led the league in penalty minutes, twice as a Maple Leaf and two times as a Black Hawk.

Gus Mortson led the NHL in penalty minutes, in both his first and fifth season in the league, as a member of the Toronto Maple Leafs. Mortson had 133 minutes in his rookie year of 1946-47 and 142 minutes in 1950-51. He was then dealt to the Chicago Black Hawks in September of 1952, where he again led the league in penalty minutes for another two seasons. In 1953-54, he recorded a league-leading 132 minutes in penalties and in 1956-57, he led the penalty parade for the season with 147 minutes.

13. The Montreal Canadiens received four players as compensation for me in a trade with the Los Angeles Kings in November of 1971.

Rogie Vachon's days as a Montreal Canadien were numbered once Ken Dryden arrived. Vachon was dealt by Montreal to the Los Angeles Kings on November 4, 1971. In return, the Canadiens received Dale Hoganson, Noel Price, Doug Robinson and goaltender Denis DeJordy.

14. I was obtained by the Buffalo Sabres from the Edmonton Oilers in exchange for Barrie Moore and Craig Millar.

In what can only be seen as a one-sided trade, Buffalo obtained high-scoring left winger Miroslav Satan from the Edmonton Oilers on March 18, 1997 for left winger Barrie Moore and defenseman Craig Millar. Satan has established himself as a scoring force since the trade. Both Moore and Millar have spent as much time in the minors as in the NHL since being dealt to Edmonton. They had both moved on to other teams by 1999.

15. I accompanied Ray Bourque in his trade from the Boston Bruins to the Colorado Avalanche.

Dave Andreychuk was traded, along with Ray Bourque, to the Colorado Avalanche from the Boston Bruins on March 6, 2000. The Bruins received Brian Rolston, Martin Grenier, Sami Pahlsson and a first round selection in the 2000 Entry Draft, which they used to obtain Martin Samuelsson. Andreychuk moved on, signing as a free agent with Buffalo, in July of 2000. He later signed on as a free agent with Tampa Bay in July of 2001.

16. I was traded to the Montreal Canadiens in exchange for Doug Harvey in 1961.

Lou Fontinato had completed his seventh season as an enforcer on the New York Rangers' blue line, when he was dealt to the Montreal Canadiens in 1961 in exchange for multiple Norris Trophy winner Doug Harvey. Fontinato was with the Canadiens for two seasons until a neck injury ended his playing career in March of 1963.

17. I was loaned to the Minnesota North Stars as a replacement for Bill Masterton, who had died as a result of an injury suffered in a game in January of 1968.

Bronco Horvath saw action with all of the Original Six teams, except Detroit, in the eight seasons between 1955-56 and 1962-63. Horvath's most successful season was in 1959-60, when he finished second to Bobby Hull in the scoring race while playing with the Boston Bruins. Horvath then ended up in the Leafs' minor system in 1963, playing largely with the Rochester Americans of the American Hockey League. After Masterton's tragic death, Toronto loaned him to Minnesota on January 21, 1968, hoping to be able to negotiate a trade with the North Stars. Horvath played in fourteen games, recording a goal and six assists for seven points in his first NHL action in five years. When a trade could not be agreed upon between Toronto and Minnesota, he was returned to Rochester of the American League on February 27, 1968.

18. I am the only player to be traded during a Calder Trophy-winning season.

Eddie Litzenberger is the only Calder Trophy recipient who skated with two teams during his winning season. Litzenberger began the 1954-55 season as a member of the Montreal Canadiens, but after twenty-nine games was traded to Chicago on December 10, 1954. Litzenberger went on to record forty points in his remaining forty-four games with the Black Hawks and was awarded the Calder Trophy for his outstanding rookie season.

19. I am the last player to be selected to the NHL First All-Star Team after having been traded during the season.

John LeClair was dealt from the Montreal Canadiens to the Philadelphia Flyers in February of 1995. LeClair was later selected as the First All-Star left winger for the 1994-95 season.

20. I am the last NHL player to be traded during the same season in which I was the penalty minute leader.

Matthew Barnaby was the penalty leader with 265 minutes in the 2000-01 season. Barnaby had 168 minutes in 47 games played with Pittsburgh, when he was dealt to Tampa Bay on February 1, 2001. Barnaby went on to pick up 97 minutes in penalties in his 29 games with the Tampa Bay Lightning.

SECOND PERIOD
THE AMATEUR/ENTRY DRAFT

1. Name the only NHL Entry Draft where each of the top three picks has gone on to play on a Stanley Cup winner.

The top three picks of the 1984 Entry Draft have all played on a Stanley Cup-winning team.

1984 Entry Draft

Selection	Player	Selected By	Stanley Cup Team(s)
1	Mario Lemieux	Pittsburgh	Pittsburgh Penguins 1991, 1992
2	Kirk Muller	New Jersey	Montreal Canadiens 1993
3	Ed Olczyk	Chicago	New York Rangers 1994

2. Name the last NHL team to have traded away the number one selection in the NHL Entry Draft on three separate occasions, prior to the draft selections taking place.

The Florida Panthers have traded away the number one selection overall on three separate occasions. The first time was in 1998, when Florida traded their first overall pick to the San Jose Sharks, who then traded it to the Tampa Bay Lightning. The Lightning selected Vincent Lecavalier. At the 2002 Entry Draft, Florida exchanged places with the Columbus Blue Jackets, who selected Rick Nash number one overall. Florida then selected Jay Bouwmeester as the third overall pick. The Panthers did a similar trade in the 2003 draft, giving up the number one overall pick to Pittsburgh, who selected Mark-Andre Fleury. As part of the trade, Florida selected Nathan Horton with the number three pick.

3. Name the two players who were selected third and fourth overall by Boston in the 1970 Amateur Draft and went on to become teammates on a Stanley Cup winner in Philadelphia.

Rick MacLeish was selected fourth overall by the Bruins in the 1970 Amateur Draft. He was sent to Philadelphia, along with Danny Schock, in return for Mike Walton in 1971. MacLeish was a stand out on both Stanley Cup-winning teams for Philadelphia in 1973-74 and 1974-75. Also in the 1970 Amateur Draft, Boston selected Reggie Leach third overall. The Bruins traded him to California in February of 1972. Leach was then picked up by the Flyers in a trade with California in May of 1974. Leach went on to play for the 1974-75 Stanley Cup champion Flyers.

4. The Flin Flon Bombers had seven players selected in the first round of the NHL Amateur Draft between 1970 and 1974. How many of them can you name?

Flin Flon, Manitoba, was a hotbed of hockey prospects in the early 1970s. The Flin Flon Bombers had seven players selected as first round picks in the NHL Amateur Draft during those years. The most famous hockey native of Flin Flon, Bobby Clarke, was selected seventeenth overall by Philadelphia in the second round of the 1969 Amateur Draft.

First Round Amateur Draft 1970-1974 - Selections from Flin-Flon

Year	Drafted	Player	Selected By
1970	3	Reggie Leach	Boston Bruins
1970	5	Ray Martyniuk	Montreal Canadiens
1971	4	Gene Carr	St. Louis Blues
1971	7	Chuck Arnason	Montreal Canadiens
1973	7	Blaine Stoughton	Pittsburgh Penguins
1974	5	Cam Connor	Montreal Canadiens
1974	6	Doug Hicks	Minnesota North Stars

5. Name Winnipeg's first ever selection in the NHL Entry Draft. (Hint: This player went on to lead the NHL in penalties in his rookie season.)

The Winnipeg Jets selected Jimmy Mann as their first selection, nineteenth overall, in the 1979 Entry Draft. This tough right winger from the Sherbrooke Beavers stepped right into the Jets' lineup, playing in 72 games in Winnipeg's first NHL season of 1979-80. While he recorded just 8 points, he racked up 287 minutes in penalties as an NHL rookie.

6. Name the four players on the 2002 Canadian Olympic team who had each been the first selection in an NHL Entry Draft.

Mario Lemieux, Owen Nolan, Eric Lindros and Ed Jovanovski were selected first overall in 1984, 1990, 1991 and 1994 respectively. They were all members of Team Canada in the 2002 Olympic Winter Games.

7. Name the three players from the London Knights junior team who had each been the first selection in an NHL Entry Draft.

Player	Selected By	Draft Year
Rick Green	Washington Capitals	1976
Rob Ramage	Colorado Rockies	1979
Rick Nash	Columbus Blue Jackets	2002

8. In which Amateur Draft year were two players selected who both went on to win the Art Ross Trophy at some point in their careers?

The first two selections of the 1971 Amateur Draft went on to become stars of the league. Guy Lafleur was selected first overall by the Montreal Canadiens and included among his many achievements three consecutive Art Ross wins for the seasons 1975-76 through 1977-78.

Marcel Dionne was picked second overall by the Detroit Red Wings. Dionne moved on to the Los Angeles Kings in 1975, where he won his lone Art Ross Trophy in 1979-80. Dionne and Lafleur were teammates on the New York Rangers in 1988-89. Both players have been inducted into the Hockey Hall of Fame.

9. What is the earliest year of the Entry Draft from which all of the top three selections were still playing in the 2002-03 NHL season?

The 1987 Entry Draft saw Pierre Turgeon, Brendan Shanahan and Glen Wesley selected in the first three spots respectively. In 2002-03, Turgeon was playing for the Dallas Stars; Shanahan was with the Detroit Red Wings; and Glen Wesley split the 2002-03 season between the Carolina Hurricanes and the Toronto Maple Leafs.

10. Name the four players selected ahead of Jaromir Jagr in the 1990 Entry Draft.

Selection	Player	Drafted By
1	Owen Nolan	Quebec Nordiques
2	Petr Nedved	Vancouver Canucks
3	Keith Primeau	Detroit Red Wings
4	Mike Ricci	Philadelphia Flyers

11. Name the two individuals who were chosen first overall in an NHL Entry Draft during the 1990s, but never played a single game with the team which selected them.

Eric Lindros was selected first overall in the 1991 Entry Draft by the Quebec Nordiques, while Bryan Berard went to the Ottawa Senators as the first player chosen in the Entry Draft in 1995. Neither of these players ever suited up with the team that selected them.

12. Name the four sets of brothers to have both been selected in the top five picks of their NHL Entry Draft.

In 1999, brothers Daniel and Henrik Sedin were chosen second and third overall by the Vancouver Canucks. Scott Niedermayer was chosen third overall by the New Jersey Devils in the 1991 Entry Draft . His brother, Rob, was selected fifth overall by the Florida Panthers in the 1993 Entry Draft. The 1983 Entry Draft saw Hartford pick Sylvain Turgeon second overall, while four years later the Buffalo Sabres opted for his brother, Pierre, as the top pick in the 1987 Draft. Both Wayne and Dave Babych also went in the top five selections. Wayne was chosen third by St. Louis in 1978, while the 1980 Draft saw Dave selected second, going to Winnipeg.

13. Name the two individuals selected first overall in an NHL Entry Draft prior to 1996, who were still skating in 2002-03 with the same franchise that had drafted them.

Mario Lemieux was selected first overall by the Pittsburgh Penguins in 1984. Mike Modano went to the Minnesota North Stars (now Dallas Stars) in the 1988 Entry Draft. They are the only two individuals chosen first overall prior to 1996 to still be playing with the team that selected them in the Entry Draft.

14. How many individuals were selected first overall in the NHL Amateur/Entry Draft and have also won the Calder Trophy?

There have been six individuals selected number one overall in the Amateur/Entry Draft that have later gone on to win the Calder Trophy to the end of 2002-03.

Player	Draft Year (Team)	Calder-Winning Season
Gilbert Perreault	1970 (Sabres)	1970-71 (Sabres)
Denis Potvin	1973 (Islanders)	1973-74 (Islanders
Bobby Smith	1978 (North Stars)	1978-79 (North Stars)
Dale Hawerchuk	1981 (Jets)	1981-82 (Jets)
Mario Lemieux	1984 (Penguins)	1984-85 (Penguins)
Bryan Berard	1995 (Senators)	1996-97 (Islanders)

15. Name the four individuals who were chosen by Vancouver as their first selections in the Canucks' first four Amateur Drafts.

Vancouver Canucks' First Selections - NHL Amateur Draft 1970-73

Year	Selected	Player	Amateur Club
1970	2	Dale Tallon	Toronto Marlboros
1971	3	Jocelyn Guevremont	Montreal Jr. Canadiens
1972	3	Don Lever	Niagara Falls Flyers
1973	3	Dennis Ververgaert	London Knights.

16. Name the only year in which three of the first five picks in the NHL Entry Draft were American-born players.

The 1983 Entry Draft was the only year in which this has happened. Brian Lawton was born in New Brunswick, New Jersey, and was selected first by the Minnesota North Stars. Lawton was the first American-born player to be chosen number one overall in the Draft. Pat LaFontaine, whose birthplace was St. Louis, Missouri, was picked third overall by the New York Islanders. Goaltender Tom Barrasso, born in Boston, Massachusetts, was selected fifth overall by the Buffalo Sabres.

17. Name the brothers who were both first round selections as defensemen from the North Bay Centennials, in separate NHL Entry Drafts.

Derian and Kevin Hatcher were both first round selections in their separate NHL Entry Drafts. While the Hatcher brothers are natives of Detroit, Michigan, both played junior hockey with the North Bay Centennials. Kevin was selected seventeenth overall by Washington in the 1984 Entry Draft, while Derian was selected eighth overall in 1990 by the Minnesota North Stars.

18. Name the first Canadian-born player to be selected by the Atlanta Thrashers with their opening pick in the NHL Entry Draft.

Braydon Coburn, who was born in Calgary, Alberta, is the first Canadian-born player to have been selected by the Atlanta Thrashers with their opening pick in the Entry Draft.

Atlanta Thrashers' First Entry-Draft Selections 1999-2003

Year	Selected	Player	Birthplace
1999	1	Patrik Stefan	Pribram, Czechoslovakia
2000	2	Dany Heatley	Freiburg, West Germany
2001	1	Ilya Kovalchuk	Tver, USSR
2002	2	Kari Lehtonen	Helsinki, Finland
2003	8	Braydon Coburn	Calgary, Alberta

19. Name the highest draft selection ever made for a goaltender by the Los Angeles Kings in the Entry Draft.

Jamie Storr was selected seventh overall by the Los Angeles Kings in the 1994 Entry Draft. Storr saw action in 205 regular season games and 5 playoff games with the Kings from 1994-95 through the 2002-03 season.

20. Name the four retired NHL players who had sons selected in the first round of the 2003 NHL Entry Draft.

Former NHL players Kent Nilsson, J.P. Parise, Steve Tambellini and Mike Eaves all had sons selected in the first round of the 2003 Entry Draft held in Nashville.

Selection	Player	Amateur Club	Selected By
15	Robert Nilsson	Leksand (Sweden)	New York Islanders
17	Zach Parise	University of North Dakota	New Jersey Devils
27	Jeff Tambellini	University of Michigan	Los Angeles Kings
29	Patrick Eaves	Boston College	Ottawa Senators

THIRD PERIOD - TRADES

1. When did an NHL team trade two players who were currently First Team All-Stars in the same deal?

In July of 1957, the Detroit Red Wings' general manager, Jack Adams, dealt goalie Glenn Hall and left winger Ted Lindsay to the Chicago Black Hawks. Both players were members of the 1956-57 NHL First All-Star team. Lindsay was traded as punishment for attempting to start a players' association. The young goaltender Hall had difficulties with Adams in his final season with the Red Wings.

2. How many players were involved in the largest single trade in NHL history?

There were ten players exchanged between the Toronto Maple Leafs and the Calgary Flames in a blockbuster trade announced on January 2, 1992. Heading to Toronto from Calgary were: Doug Gilmour, Jamie Macoun, Ric Nattress, Kent Manderville and Rick Wamsley. In return, Toronto sent Gary Leeman, Alexander Godynyuk, Jeff Reese, Michel Petit and Craig Berube to the Flames.

3. Name the three players that the Los Angeles Kings received when they traded Wayne Gretzky to the St. Louis Blues in February of 1996.

Craig Johnson, Patrice Tardif and Roman Vopat were received in exchange for Gretzky during this trade. Only Craig Johnson still plays in the NHL, having just completed his eighth season as a member of the Los Angeles Kings in 2002-03.

4. Name the veteran goalies who saw their first NHL action with Toronto in the Original Six era and were exchanged for each other in August of 1976.

Cesare Maniago was traded to the Vancouver Canucks by the Minnesota North Stars in exchange for Gary Smith on August 23, 1976. Maniago, who had seen action in the Original Six with Toronto, Montreal and New York, had played nine seasons with the North Stars and finished out his career with two final seasons with Vancouver. Smith, who had also played in the Original Six era with Toronto, went on to skate with Oakland/California, Chicago, Vancouver, Minnesota, Washington, and Winnipeg in the NHL. He also was a member of Indianapolis and Winnipeg in the WHA.

5. Name the two individuals who were traded in separate deals for Guy Carbonneau.

Guy Carbonneau played for twelve complete seasons with the Montreal Canadiens, where he won three Selke Trophies and captained the team for several years. He was dealt to St. Louis in exchange for Jim Montgomery in August of 1994. Montgomery went on to play a total of five games for the Montreal Canadiens before being claimed on waivers by Philadelphia in 1995. Carbonneau only put in one season with the St. Louis Blues before he was dealt to the Dallas Stars in exchange for Paul Broten in October of 1995. Broten played his final seventeen games in the NHL with St. Louis in 1995-96, while Carbonneau went on to play five more solid seasons of hockey with the Dallas Stars. He added a third Stanley Cup in 1999 to complement the two he had won previously with the Montreal Canadiens.

6. Name the only Stastny brother to be involved in an NHL trade.

Peter Stastny was the only Stastny brother to be involved in a trade in the National Hockey League. All three originally were members of the Quebec Nordiques. Peter and Anton signed in 1980-81 and older brother Marian joined them for 1981-82. Anton played his entire NHL career with the Quebec Nordiques. Marian was a teammate with his two brothers through 1985, when he signed as a free agent with the Toronto Maple Leafs. He played one final NHL season with the Leafs before heading back to Europe to play hockey. Peter was a member of the Quebec Nordiques through 1989-90, when he was dealt to New Jersey for Craig Wolanin and future considerations (Randy Velischek). Peter did play for a third NHL franchise, the St. Louis Blues, when he signed on as a free agent in 1994.

7. How did the Vancouver Canucks acquire Markus Naslund?

Vancouver Canuck general manager, Pat Quinn, pulled off a very lopsided deal in March of 1996 by acquiring Markus Naslund from the Pittsburgh Penguins in exchange for Alek Stojanov. Stojanov, a Windsor native, had been selected seventh overall in the 1991 Entry Draft, the same year in which Naslund went sixteenth to the Pittsburgh Penguins. Stojanov went on to play forty-five games with the Pittsburgh Penguins over the next two seasons scoring just two goals, while Naslund's career began to hit stride as he recorded forty-one points in 1996-97 with Vancouver.

8. Who accompanied Wayne Gretzky in a WHA trade from the Indianapolis Racers to the Edmonton Oilers in November of 1978?

The Indianapolis Racers traded Wayne Gretzky, Peter Driscoll and goaltender Eddie Mio to the Edmonton Oilers in exchange for seven hundred thousand dollars on November 2, 1978. While everyone is familiar with Gretzky's accomplishments, Driscoll also played a significant role for the Oilers, recording forty points in the remaining regular season games and seven more in the playoffs. Eddie Mio played in a total of twenty-five games between the regular season and playoffs with the Oilers in that last WHA season. Both Driscoll and Mio played with Edmonton in the Oilers' first two NHL seasons.

9. To which NHL team was Ed Belfour dealt in a trade by the Chicago Blackhawks?

Ed Belfour, who was about to become an unrestricted free agent, was traded to the San Jose Sharks by Chicago in January of 1997. The Blackhawks received Chris Terreri, Ulf Dahlen and Michal Sykora from the Sharks in return. Belfour only played in thirteen games with the Sharks before signing as a free agent with Dallas in July of 1997.

10. Name the two goaltenders traded from the Montreal Canadiens to the New York Islanders in the same deal in June of 1972.

The Montreal Canadiens sent the New York Islanders a package of players for cash on June 26, 1972. This included goaltenders Glenn "Chico" Resch and Denis Dejordy. Resch would not play for the Islanders until their second season of 1973-74. He then went on to play the majority of their games in the late seventies, winning the Stanley Cup in 1980. He moved on through Colorado with the Rockies and was a member of both the New Jersey Devils and the Philadelphia Flyers prior to his retirement in 1987. When traded to New York, Dejordy was near the end of his career. He had been in net for Chicago, Los Angeles and Montreal to this point. The Islanders traded Dejordy to the Detroit Red Wings prior to the beginning of the 1972-73 season, where Dejordy saw action for two final seasons before retiring in 1974.

11. How did Jaromir Jagr become a Washington Capital?

The Pittsburgh Penguins traded Jagr, along with Frantisek Kucera, to the Washington Capitals in return for Kris Beech, Michal Sivek and Ross Lupaschuk in July of 2001.

12. How did the New York Islanders obtain Butch Goring?

The New York Islanders obtained Butch Goring in March of 1980 to bolster their lineup for the Stanley Cup playoffs. The Islanders sent Billy Harris and Dave Lewis to the Los Angeles Kings as compensation for Goring. The trade turned out well for the Islanders, as they captured their first of four consecutive Stanley Cups that playoff year.

13. Name the three players that the Montreal Canadiens traded to acquire Frank Mahovlich.

The Detroit Red Wings obtained Guy Charron, Bill Collins and Mickey Redmond from the Montreal Canadiens in exchange for Frank Mahovlich on January 13, 1971.

14. Who did the Edmonton Oilers receive from the Boston Bruins in return for Andy Moog in March of 1988?

Andy Moog joined the Canadian Olympic team for 1987-88 rather than return to the Edmonton Oilers as backup to Grant Fuhr. After the Olympics, the Oilers shipped him to Boston in return for goaltender Bill Ranford, forward Geoff Courtnall and a second round draft pick in the 1988 Entry Draft. Moog ended up facing his former Oilers in both the 1988 and 1990 Stanley Cup final.

15. Name the two players given up in separate deals by the Detroit Red Wings to obtain Igor Larionov.

The Detroit Red Wings traded for Larionov on two separate occasions. The first time was on October 24, 1995, when the Red Wings dealt Ray Sheppard to the San Jose Sharks in return for Larionov. After five seasons, which included two Stanley Cups with the Red Wings, Larionov signed as a free agent with the Florida Panthers in July of 2000. He was returned to the Red Wings in December of that same year when they traded Yan Golubovsky to the Panthers.

16. Name the four players that the Toronto Maple Leafs sent to the Chicago Black Hawks in September of 1952, to acquire future Hall of Fame goaltender Harry Lumley.

The Leafs sent forwards Cal Gardner and Ray Hannigan, defenseman Gus Mortson and goalie Al Rollins to the Black Hawks in return for goaltender Harry Lumley on September 11, 1952.

17. Name the three forwards involved in a three-way deal between the Colorado Avalanche, the New Jersey Devils and the New York Islanders in October of 1995.

The New Jersey Devils sent Claude Lemieux to the New York Islanders for Steve Thomas. The Islanders turned around and traded Claude Lemieux to the Colorado Avalanche in exchange for Wendel Clark.

18. Name the two veteran NHL goaltenders who were traded for each other in July of 1980.

Gilles Gilbert was traded by the Boston Bruins to the Detroit Red Wings in exchange for Rogie Vachon on July 15, 1980. Gilbert, who had played net in eleven seasons with Minnesota and Boston, backstopped three more with the Detroit Red Wings. Vachon had seen action in fourteen NHL seasons with Montreal, Los Angeles and Detroit. He played his final two seasons with the Boston Bruins.

19. These two players, who were both selected second overall in an NHL Entry Draft, played on the Canadian Olympic team in 1998 and 2002. They were once traded for each other.

Chris Pronger and Brendan Shanahan were traded for each other on July 27, 1995. Shanahan had been a second overall selection by New Jersey in 1987. He moved on to St. Louis as a free agent in 1991. Pronger had been chosen second overall by the Hartford Whalers in the 1993 Entry Draft, where he played for two seasons before he was shipped to St. Louis in exchange for Shanahan. Both Shanahan and Pronger played for Canada at the Olympic Winter Games in 1998 and 2002.

20. Name the five captains of 1967-68 NHL teams who were traded prior to the beginning of the 1968-69 season.

Four of the NHL's six new teams in 1967-68 dealt away their captains prior to the beginning of the next season. Philadelphia captain Lou Angotti was traded to the St. Louis Blues in June of 1968. St. Louis immediately dealt him to Pittsburgh in return for Penguin captain Ab McDonald. Minnesota captain, Bob Woytowich, was sent to the Pittsburgh Penguins for a draft choice, prior to the beginning of the 1968-69 season. Oakland captain Bob Baun was traded to the Detroit Red Wings in a multi-player deal in May of 1968. The Chicago Black Hawks also traded their captain, Pierre Pilote, to the Toronto Maple Leafs in exchange for Jim Pappin that spring.

Owen Nolan was traded to the Toronto Maple Leafs in March of 2003.

PHOTO REPLAY

1. How many players have been selected first in an NHL Amateur/Entry Draft since 1969 and have also played on the Toronto Maple Leafs?

Owen Nolan is the seventh player to have been selected first in an NHL Amateur/Entry Draft and also play for the Toronto Maple Leafs.

First Selections in NHL Entry Draft to play for Toronto

Draft Year	Player	Selected By	First Leaf Season
1972	Billy Harris	New York Islanders	1981-82
1977	Dale McCourt	Detroit Red Wings	1983-84
1979	Rob Ramage	Colorado Rockies	1989-90
1985	Wendel Clark	Toronto Maple Leafs	1985-86
1989	Mats Sundin	Quebec Nordiques	1994-95
1990	Owen Nolan	Quebec Nordiques	2002-03
1995	Bryan Berard	Ottawa Senators	1998-99

2. Name the two players, other than Owen Nolan and Mats Sundin, who were selected in the top three in an NHL Entry Draft and were members of the Toronto Maple Leafs in the 2003 playoffs.

Leaf defensemen Glen Wesley and Aki Berg were both selected third overall in an NHL Entry Draft. Wesley was chosen in the 1987 Draft by Boston and Berg was selected by Los Angeles in the 1995 Draft.

3. Did Owen Nolan ever play for the Colorado Avalanche?

Owen Nolan was entering his sixth NHL season with the franchise, their first in Colorado, when he was traded to the San Jose Sharks. Nolan suited up for the Avalanche for a total of nine games, scoring eight points to open the 1995-96 season, when he was dealt to San Jose in return for Sandis Ozolinsh.

4. How did the Maple Leafs obtain Owen Nolan from the Sharks?

Toronto traded center Alyn McCauley, Brad Boyes (the Leafs' first selection in the 2000 Entry Draft) and their first-round pick in the 2003 Entry Draft to San Jose in exchange for Nolan on March 5, 2003.

Thanks for the Memories

The earliest details of the game of hockey are now dependent on what has been handed down over the years. The pioneers of the NHL have passed on and with them much of the league's early history. Franchises that once filled arenas with fans are now no longer part of the system. The old buildings of the Original Six have been replaced by new entertainment complexes. Hockey has gone big business. However, the Hall of Fame carries on much of the history by preserving the relics of the past and passing on any available knowledge of bygone traditions to many interested fans.

FIRST PERIOD
THEY DON'T PLAY HERE ANYMORE

1. Which former NHL franchise played the fewest number of games in the league?

The Montreal Wanderers were charter members of the NHL that began play in December of 1917. The team had only played four games when their arena was destroyed by fire in January of 1918. The Wanderers withdrew from the league with a 1-3-0 record. They had won their season opener against Toronto, but lost to the Canadiens once and were twice defeated by the Ottawa Senators. After the Wanderers left the league, one defaulted win was credited to both the Montreal Canadiens and the Toronto Arenas to balance the schedule for the remainder of the season. The resulting Montreal Wanderers' official record is one win and five losses, despite the fact they only hit the ice for four matches.

2. Name the only individual who played in a hockey game with all five of the charter franchises of the National Hockey League.

Dave Ritchie was the property of the Quebec Bulldogs of the National Hockey Association which became the National Hockey League for the 1917-18 season. Quebec decided not to ice a team that year, so Ritchie began his season with the Montreal Wanderers. After the Wanderers withdrew from the league, Ritchie was picked up by the Ottawa Senators for the remainder of the 1917-18 season. He then signed with the Toronto Arenas during the 1918-19 season. Quebec decided to take part in the National Hockey League in 1919-20, so his rights were transferred back to the Bulldogs. The Quebec franchise relocated to Hamilton for the following season, but Ritchie was traded to the Montreal Canadiens where he played in 1920-21. Ritchie then became a referee for three seasons from 1921-22 to 1923-24. He briefly returned to action with the Canadiens in both 1924-25 and 1925-26.

3. Name the three west coast teams that won the Stanley Cup.

The 1915 Vancouver Millionaires, the 1917 Seattle Metropolitans and the 1925 Victoria Cougars were all Stanley Cup champions.

4. Name the two defunct NHL franchises that won the Stanley Cup.

Both the original Ottawa Senators franchise and the Montreal Maroons won the Stanley Cup. The Ottawa Senators captured the trophy as an NHL franchise in 1920, 1921, 1923 and 1927. The team left Ottawa in 1934 for St. Louis and played its last NHL season as the Eagles in 1934-35. The Montreal Maroons won the Stanley Cup in 1926 and 1935. Their last season of NHL action was 1937-38.

5. Name the five players who won the Hart Trophy with a defunct NHL franchise.

Hart Trophy Winners with Defunct NHL Franchises

Player	Team	Season
Frank Nighbor	Ottawa Senators	1923-24
Billy Burch	Hamilton Tigers	1924-25
Nels Stewart	Montreal Maroons	1925-26, 1929-30
Roy Worters	New York Americans	1928-29
Tom Anderson	Brooklyn Americans	1941-42

6. Which team entered the NHL with the New York Islanders for the 1972-73 season?

The Atlanta Flames franchise first hit the ice in 1972. They relocated to Calgary in 1980.

7. Who was the first coach of the Winnipeg Jets in the WHA?

Bobby Hull served as player-coach for the Winnipeg Jets from the beginning of the WHA in 1972-73 into their third season. Hull passed the coaching duties to Rudy Pilous in the 1974-75 season.

8. When did a WHA franchise first defeat an NHL franchise?

The Houston Aeros of the WHA defeated the St. Louis Blues of the NHL by a score of 5-3 in an exhibition game played on September 26, 1974. This was the first of sixty-seven pre-season matches between teams from the rival leagues. It is interesting to note that the WHA teams had a winning record of 33-27-7 in these exhibitions against NHL opponents from 1974 to 1978.

9. When was an NHL team first located in the state of Ohio?

The Cleveland Barons tied the Los Angeles Kings 2-2 in their home opener at the Coliseum on Wednesday, October 6, 1976. The California Golden Seals had relocated to Cleveland for the 1976-77 season. The franchise only survived in this city for two seasons before folding. The Cleveland players were transferred to the struggling Minnesota North Stars in 1978. Ohio would be without an NHL franchise until the Columbus Blue Jackets arrived to begin play in the 2000-01 season.

10. What is the highest point total ever recorded in one season by a player with a defunct NHL franchise?

Dennis Maruk of the Cleveland Barons recorded twenty-eight goals and fifty assists for seventy-eight points in eighty games during the 1976-77 NHL season.

11. Name the only four players to have won a WHA scoring race.

Real Cloutier, Andre Lacroix, Marc Tardif, Mike Walton.

WHA Scoring Leaders

Year	Player	Team	GP	G	A	PTS
1972-73	Andre Lacroix	Philadelphia Blazers	78	50	74	124
1973-74	Mike Walton	Minnesota Fighting Saints	78	57	60	117
1974-75	Andre Lacroix	San Diego Mariners	78	41	106	147
1975-76	Marc Tardif	Quebec Nordiques	81	71	77	148
1976-77	Real Cloutier	Quebec Nordiques	76	66	75	141
1977-78	Marc Tardif	Quebec Nordiques	78	65	89	154
1978-79	Real Cloutier	Quebec Nordiques	77	75	54	129

12. Which franchise won the most championships in the World Hockey Association?

The Winnipeg Jets won the Avco World Trophy three of the seven times it was presented to the WHA champions. Winnipeg was first awarded the Avco Cup in 1975-76. They then repeated as champions in the last two years of the league's existence, 1977-78 and 1978-79. The Houston Aeros were the only other WHA team to win the Avco Cup on more than one occasion, when they won back-to-back championships in 1973-74 and 1974-75. The other two winners of the WHA championship were the 1972-73 New England Whalers and the 1976-77 Quebec Nordiques.

13. Name the four defensemen from Team Canada '72 who saw their final NHL action with a franchise that has since relocated.

Player	1972 NHL Team	Final NHL Team
Don Awrey	Boston Bruins	Colorado Rockies, 1978-79
Gary Bergman	Detroit Red Wings	Kansas City Scouts 1975-76
Serge Savard	Montreal Canadiens	Winnipeg Jets, 1982-83
Rod Seiling	New York Rangers	Atlanta Flames, 1978-79

14. Name the two players who reached 100 points with the Hartford Whalers in 1979-80.

Mike Rogers and Blaine Stoughton finished fifth and eighth in the NHL scoring race in 1979-80. Rogers recorded 44 goals and 61 assists for 105 points, while Stoughton recorded 56 goals and 44 assists for 100 points.

This is the only time that the franchise had two players record 100 or more points in a single season, from their entry into the NHL in 1979 until the franchise transferred to Carolina in 1997.

15. Who is the only member of the Minnesota North Stars to have been awarded the Bill Masterton Trophy?

Al MacAdam of the Minnesota North Stars was presented with the Bill Masterton Trophy in 1980. The trophy recognizes the player who best exemplifies the qualities of perseverance, sportsmanship and dedication to hockey. The trophy is awarded in memory of Bill Masterton, a Minnesota North Star, who died as a result of injuries suffered in an NHL game in January of 1968. Al MacAdam is the only player from that franchise to have been awarded this trophy to date.

16. Name the individual who played all of his NHL games (over one thousand) with the Winnipeg Jets.

Thomas Steen played a total of 950 regular season and 56 playoff games, all with the Winnipeg Jets, between 1981-82 and 1994-95. Steen's number 25 is one of only two numbers retired by the Winnipeg Jets to recognize his outstanding contribution to the franchise. Winnipeg has also retired number 9, to honor Bobby Hull.

17. Name the three individuals who played goal for the Nordiques in their final NHL season in Quebec.

Stephane Fiset, Garth Snow and Jocelyn Thibault all saw game action in both the regular season and the playoffs during the Nordiques' final season of 1994-95, before the team moved on to Colorado as the Avalanche.

18. Who were the first and last players to represent the Quebec Nordiques in an NHL All-Star game?

Real Cloutier was the only skater from the expansion Nordiques playing in the 1980 All-Star Game held in Detroit. He recorded a goal and an assist for the Wales Conference in their 6-3 win over the Campbell Conference. Joe Sakic was the last player to represent Quebec at an All-Star match. Sakic netted a goal and two assists for the Eastern All-Stars, as they defeated the West 9-8 at Madison Square Garden in 1994.

19. How many playoff series did the Winnipeg Jets win as an NHL team?

The Jets won only two playoff series during their seventeen NHL seasons in Winnipeg. Their first playoff success was in the 1985 Smythe Division semi-final, when they defeated the Calgary Flames three games to one in a best-of-five series. The Jets were then swept in four straight games by the Edmonton Oilers in the Smythe Division final. In 1987, the Jets again defeated Calgary in the Smythe Division semi-final, only to be swept once more by the Edmonton Oilers in the Smythe Division final.

20. Name the only Canadian city to have had an NHL franchise, but never win the Stanley Cup.

The Hamilton Tigers were members of the National Hockey League for five seasons from 1920-21 to 1924-25. However, the city of Hamilton has never had a Stanley Cup-winning team. NHL franchises from Calgary, Edmonton, Montreal, Ottawa and Toronto have all won the Stanley Cup. While Quebec, Winnipeg and Vancouver have never seen their NHL franchises capture the trophy, all have been home to at least one Stanley Cup champion prior to the formation of the National Hockey League. Kenora and Victoria have also had a Cup winner, even though they have never had an NHL franchise.

SECOND PERIOD - THE HALL OF FAME

1. Name the two Hall of Famers who both played in their last game with the Montreal Canadiens in November of 1984.

Steve Shutt was traded by Montreal to the Los Angeles Kings for future considerations on November 19, 1984. He would go on to play in sixty-two games with the Kings through that season before retiring. On November 26, 1984, Guy Lafleur announced his retirement as a player with the Montreal Canadiens. Lafleur remained retired as a player until the 1988-89 season, when he returned to the NHL with the New York Rangers.

2. Name the two Hall of Famers who were both claimed by the Toronto Maple Leafs at the Intra-League Draft on June 10, 1964.

The Toronto Maple Leafs were able to claim both goaltender Terry Sawchuk from the Detroit Red Wings and left winger Dickie Moore from the Montreal Canadiens on June 10, 1964. While Sawchuk would make a major contribution to the Maple Leafs over the next three seasons, including his integral part in the 1967 Stanley Cup, Moore would only play in a total of forty-three games through 1964-65 before retiring for a second time. Moore did return to the NHL once more with the 1967-68 St. Louis Blues.

3. How many Hall of Famers were selected by the six new NHL teams in the 1967 Expansion Draft?

There were six future Hall of Famers selected in the Expansion Draft of 1967. Goaltenders Glenn Hall, Bernie Parent and Terry Sawchuk all moved to new teams. Hall was selected by the St. Louis Blues from the Chicago Black Hawks; Sawchuk by the Los Angeles Kings from the Maple Leafs; and Parent by the Philadelphia Flyers from the Boston Bruins. The Pittsburgh Penguins chose both Leo Boivin and Andy Bathgate from the Detroit Red Wings. Al Arbour went to the St. Louis Blues from the Toronto Maple Leafs. He would later be inducted as a builder into the Hall of Fame based on his coaching career with the New York Islanders.

4. Name the two Hall of Famers who both played their first NHL game with the Montreal Canadiens on December 16, 1950.

Jean Beliveau and Bernard "Boom-Boom" Geoffrion both played their first NHL game on December 16, 1950. Geoffrion scored the Canadiens' only goal in a 1-1 tie against the visiting New York Rangers.

5. Name the Hall of Famer who played his first NHL hockey with the Brooklyn Americans.

Harry "Whipper" Watson played forty-seven games in his rookie season with the 1941-42 Brooklyn Americans. It was the Americans' final year in the NHL and the only one where their home was identified as Brooklyn rather than New York. Watson's rights were transferred to Detroit, where he won a Stanley Cup the following season. After military service, he returned in 1945 to play with Detroit for one more season, before being dealt to Toronto where he was a member on four more Cup winners. He was traded to Chicago in December of 1954 and finished his NHL playing career with the Black Hawks in 1957.

6. Name the individual who scored an amazing thirty-seven goals in the five games he played at the 1924 Olympics.

Harry Watson, not to be confused with the player of NHL fame, was the star of the 1924 Canadian Olympic hockey team which dominated the event. The Canadians won by scores of 30-0, 22-0, 33-0 and 19-2 over Czechoslovakia, Sweden, Switzerland and Great Britain respectively. Their closest match was a 6-1 win over the United States. Five players hit double-digits in scoring for Canada, but Watson with his thirty-seven goals, was the outstanding player of the Games. This included an amazing thirteen goals scored in the single game against Switzerland. Watson saw considerable amateur senior action in the Toronto area, but never played in the NHL.

7. Name the Hall of Fame goaltender who played with a different team in each of his last four NHL seasons.

Terry Sawchuk was a key member of the Stanley Cup-winning Toronto Maple Leafs in 1966-67. He was then claimed by the Los Angeles Kings in the 1967 Expansion Draft. The Kings traded him to Detroit in 1968 and the Red Wings dealt him to the New York Rangers in 1969. He played his final season with the Rangers in 1969-70.

8. Name the four individuals selected for induction into the Hockey Hall of Fame in November of 2003.

Grant Fuhr and Pat LaFontaine were selected for induction as players into the Hall of Fame. Mike Ilitch and Brian Kilrea were chosen as builders. Grant Fuhr was a standout in goal, winning five Stanley Cups with the Edmonton Oilers. Fuhr played for six different teams over his nineteen NHL seasons. LaFontaine played with the New York Islanders, the New York Rangers and the Buffalo Sabres over fifteen seasons, before he was forced to retire due to recurring concussions. As a coach, Brian Kilrea was behind the bench for the Ottawa 67s of the Canadian Hockey League for twenty-six seasons through 2002-03. He has recorded over a thousand wins as a head coach. He guided Ottawa to a Memorial Cup championship in 1984 and again in 1999. Mike Ilitch purchased the Detroit Red Wings from the Norris family in 1982. He has been a driving force in turning around this Original Six franchise.

9. This high-scoring left winger was a member of five Stanley Cup winners in the 1920s, four with Ottawa and one with Boston.

Cy Denneny was a member of the Ottawa Senators until 1928, where he won the Stanley Cup four times in the first eleven seasons of the National Hockey League. He was then traded to Boston where he coached and also played on the first Bruins' Stanley Cup team in 1929. Denneny was the NHL's scoring leader in 1923-24 and placed second in the scoring race on five other occasions.

10. In which season did twelve future Hall of Famers skate with the Toronto Maple Leafs?

The 1964-65 Toronto Maple Leafs had twelve future members of the Hall of Fame skate with the team: Al Arbour*, George Armstrong, Andy Bathgate, Johnny Bower, Tim Horton, Red Kelly, Dave Keon, Frank Mahovlich, Dickie Moore, Bob Pulford, Terry Sawchuk and Allan Stanley. During this season, the Maple Leafs lost in the semi-final to the Montreal Canadiens. The four Maple Leaf championship teams of the 1960s boasted most of these players as members, but no other Toronto team had twelve future Hall of Famers on its roster.

*While the other eleven players were selected to the Hall of Fame based on their playing career, it should be noted that Al Arbour was selected based on his coaching accomplishments. Al Arbour's only appearance with the Maple Leafs in this season was in a single playoff game in the 1965 semi-final.

11. Name the two Hall of Famers who skated with the Montreal Wanderers during their brief playing careers in the National Hockey League.

Art Ross and Harry Hyland both played their last hockey in 1917-18, the first year of the NHL. Art Ross is the better known player of the two, achieving notoriety as the general manager of the Boston Bruins through the first thirty years of the franchise. Ross was an inductee into the Hall based on his playing career. He was a member of the Stanley Cup-winning team in Kenora in 1907 and won the Cup again in 1908 with the Montreal Wanderers. Ross played in the NHA with the Haileybury Silver Kings, the Montreal Wanderers and the Ottawa Senators. He only saw

NHL action as a player in three games with the Montreal Wanderers in 1917. Ross also coached the Wanderers during their short existence in the National Hockey League. Harry Hyland's only NHL experience was in 1917-18, scoring six goals in four games with the Wanderers and finishing the season with the Ottawa Senators, where he recorded eight more goals in thirteen games. Hyland was chosen for the Hall of Fame for an outstanding career in the National Hockey Association. This included a Stanley Cup championship with the Wanderers in 1910.

12. Which one of the three Conacher brothers was briefly a member of the Montreal Canadiens?

None of the Hall of Fame Conacher brothers, Charlie, Lionel or Roy, ever played in a single NHL game with the Canadiens. However, Lionel Conacher was briefly owned by the Habs. Conacher was a member of the 1934 Stanley Cup-winning Chicago Black Hawks, who traded him along with Leroy Goldsworthy and Roger Jenkins to the Montreal Canadiens in return for Howie Morenz, Lorne Chabot and Marty Burke on October 3, 1934. The Canadiens then turned around and dealt Conacher to the Montreal Maroons, along with the rights to Herb Cain, for McGill University star Nels Crutchfield.

13. This Hall of Famer scored seven goals in Canada's final hockey game at the 1920 Olympics.

Frank Fredrickson scored seven goals for the Winnipeg Falcons in Canada's 12-1 victory over Sweden in the gold medal match held on April 26, 1920. It is interesting to note that he attained this feat in a game that was only forty minutes in length. When Fredrickson and his teammates represented Canada at these Olympics in Belgium, hockey was included as a demonstration sport in what was actually the seventh Summer Games. Fredrickson went on to play professionally for Victoria in the Pacific Coast Hockey Association and suited up for Detroit, Boston and Pittsburgh in the NHL. Fredrickson was inducted into the Hockey Hall of Fame in 1958.

14. **All thirteen individuals who served as a head coach during the five NHL seasons between 1948-49 and 1952-53 were inducted into the Hockey Hall of Fame. How many of them can you name?**

NHL Head Coaches, 1948-49 through 1952-53

Team	Coaches
Boston Bruins	Dit Clapper, George Boucher, Lynn Patrick
Chicago Black Hawks	Charlie Conacher, Ebbie Goodfellow, Sid Abel
Detroit Red Wings	Tommy Ivan
Montreal Canadiens	Dick Irvin
New York Rangers	Frank Boucher, Lynn Patrick, Neil Colville, Bill Cook
Toronto Maple Leafs	Hap Day, Joe Primeau

15. **Who was the first American-born player to be selected to the Hockey Hall of Fame?**

Hobey Baker was one of the twelve original players selected for induction into the Hockey Hall of Fame in 1945. Baker was born in Wisahicton, Pennsylvania, in 1892. He was the star of the hockey team at Princeton University for four seasons, beginning in 1910-11. After graduation, Baker played for the St. Nicholas hockey team of the American senior ranks for two seasons, his last being in 1915-16. Hobey Baker enlisted in the war effort and became a pilot. He lived through the war, but died while testing a plane in December of 1918. An award in his name is presented annually to the top college player in the United States.

16. **Name the four Hall of Famers who all played in their final NHL All-Star game in 1980.**

Brothers Tony and Phil Esposito competed for the Campbell Conference All-Stars, while Jean Ratelle and Gordie Howe suited up for the Wales Conference All-Stars, in what would be the final NHL All-Star game for all four of these Hall of Famers. Howe's appearance in front of his long-time fans in Detroit was the highlight of the game. Howe recorded his final All-Star point with just under four minutes to go, as the Wales defeated the Campbells 6-3.

17. Name the first three individuals selected to the Hockey Hall of Fame as officials.

Chaucer Elliott, Mickey Ion and Cooper Smeaton were all inducted in 1961 as officials. Chaucer Elliott was an outstanding athlete in many sports, who was widely renowned for his hockey refereeing ability in the ten years prior to his death in 1913 at the age of 34. Cooper Smeaton began refereeing in the National Hockey Association and refereed in most of the NHL seasons between 1917-18 and 1936-37. Mickey Ion began his refereeing career in the Pacific Coast Hockey Association and later moved on to the NHL in the 1920s where he continued refereeing in the league until 1940-41.

18. These Hall of Famers both won the same two trophies and were each on several Stanley Cup winners in Montreal. They both retired as Montreal Canadiens before returning to play with the New York Rangers.

Bernie "Boom-Boom" Geoffrion and Guy Lafleur have many similarities in their careers. Both played fourteen seasons with the Montreal Canadiens. Geoffrion was on six Cup winners, while Lafleur hoisted Lord Stanley's mug on five occasions. Geoffrion received the Art Ross Trophy in both 1954-55 and 1960-61. Lafleur won it in three consecutive seasons from 1975-76 through 1977-78. Geoffrion also won the Hart Trophy as the NHL's most valuable player in 1960-61. It was Lafleur's turn to receive the honor in both 1976-77 and 1977-78. Geoffrion and Lafleur retired from playing after outstanding careers only to return to the National Hockey League as members of the New York Rangers. Geoffrion played his final two seasons in 1966-67 and 1967-68 with the Rangers, while Lafleur returned as a Ranger for one season in 1988-89, before playing his final two seasons with the Quebec Nordiques.

19. Name the seven Hall of Famers who played goal with the New York Rangers between 1945-46 and 1975-76.

For thirty-one consecutive seasons between 1945-46 and 1975-76, the New York Rangers had a future Hall of Famer in goal, for at least part of each season. These goaltenders were: Chuck Rayner, Emile Francis (inducted as a builder), Lorne "Gump" Worsley, Johnny Bower, Jacques Plante, Ed Giacomin and Terry Sawchuk.

20. Name the three Hall of Fame players who the Toronto Maple Leafs acquired in 1958.

Johnny Bower was claimed in the Inter-League Draft on June 3, 1958, from the Cleveland Barons of the American Hockey League. On that same date, the Leafs also acquired Bert Olmstead from the Montreal Canadiens in the Intra-League Draft. The third Hall of Famer who came to the Leafs that year was Allan Stanley, who was obtained through a trade with the Boston Bruins on October 8, 1958. The Leafs sent Jim Morrison to the Bruins in return. This was the first major deal orchestrated by Punch Imlach on behalf of the Leafs.

THIRD PERIOD - THE PLAYOFFS

1. Name the only three expansion teams of the post-Original Six era to win the Stanley Cup at least three times.

The New York Islanders were the first to achieve this, winning the Stanley Cup in four consecutive years from 1980 to 1983. The Edmonton Oilers hoisted the Cup on five occasions between 1984 and 1990. The New Jersey Devils are the most recent of the expansion teams to win the Cup three times. They celebrated Stanley Cup victories in 1995, 2000 and 2003.

2. Name the first two NHL teams to meet for five consecutive years in the Stanley Cup playoffs.

The Toronto Maple Leafs and the Montreal Canadiens matched up in the playoffs for five consecutive seasons from 1963 through 1967. The Leafs eliminated the Canadiens in the semi-final in both 1963 and 1964, with the Canadiens returning the favour in the semi-final of 1965 and 1966. The Leafs were victorious in 1967, winning the final series in six games. The Dallas Stars and the Edmonton Oilers more recently met for five consecutive playoffs between 1997 and 2001.

3. Name the only franchise to have faced four Canadian NHL teams in one playoff year.

The 1993 Los Angeles Kings defeated the Calgary Flames in the Smythe Division semi-final and the Vancouver Canucks in the Smythe Division final, before eliminating Toronto in the Campbell Conference final. In the Stanley Cup final, the Kings were defeated by the Montreal Canadiens.

4. Name the only two NHL teams that played in a best-of-three preliminary playoff series every year between 1975 and 1979.

The Los Angeles Kings and the Toronto Maple Leafs are the only two teams to have played in a preliminary best-of-three playoff series for five consecutive years. The series was introduced, beginning in 1975, to eliminate four of the twelve playoff teams. The best-of-three preliminary round was abandoned for the 1980 playoffs.

5. Name the last four teams to host the NHL All-Star game and follow it up with a Stanley Cup victory later that season.

Stanley Cup Champions	All-Star Game
2000-01 Colorado Avalanche	February 4, 2001 at the Pepsi Center North America 14, World 12
1993-94 New York Rangers	January 22, 1994 at Madison Square Garden East 9, West 8
1992-93 Montreal Canadiens	February 6, 1993 at the Montreal Forum Wales 16, Campbell 6
1982-83 New York Islanders	February 8, 1983 at the Nassau County Coliseum Campbell 9, Wales 3

6. The 2002-03 Carolina Hurricanes missed the playoffs after being in the Stanley Cup final the previous year. Name the three teams that had this dubious distinction in the 1990s.

The 1993-94 Los Angeles Kings and the 1998-99 Washington Capitals both failed to make the playoffs following appearances in a Stanley Cup final the year before. The 1995-96 New Jersey Devils failed to qualify for the playoffs after winning the Stanley Cup the previous year.

7. When was the only time between 1928 and 1973, that the Stanley Cup-winning game was not played in an Original Six city?

In 1969, the Montreal Canadiens defeated the St. Louis Blues in the Stanley Cup final. The fourth and final game of the series took place in St. Louis on May 4, 1969. The Stanley Cup had been won at home by the Ottawa Senators in 1927 and the Flyers won the Cup in Philadelphia in 1974. Except for the match in St. Louis, all other Stanley Cup-winning games between 1928 and 1973 took place in an Original Six city.

8. Which NHL team went to overtime in each of their opening games in three consecutive playoff series in 2003?

The Anaheim Mighty Ducks opened each of their first three playoff series with an overtime win in 2003. Paul Kariya scored in the third overtime, as the Ducks took the first game of the Western Conference quarter-final from the Red Wings 2-1. Anaheim eliminated Detroit in four straight games. Petr Sykora notched the winner in the fifth extra frame, when Anaheim defeated Dallas 4-3 to open the Conference semi-final. The Ducks took the Stars in six games in that series. Sykora repeated his overtime magic to give the Ducks a 1-0 win over Minnesota in game one of the Conference final. The Ducks went on to sweep the Wild in four games.

9. Name the only three NHL franchises to have defeated the Montreal Canadiens in a Stanley Cup final.

The Calgary Flames, the Detroit Red Wings and the Toronto Maple Leafs have all defeated the Canadiens in a final series. Calgary is the last team to accomplish this, defeating Montreal four games to two in the 1989 Stanley Cup final. Toronto eliminated the Canadiens in a Cup final in 1947, 1951 and 1967. Detroit won the Cup over the Habs in 1952, 1954 and 1955.

10. Name the only two teams to have won game seven of a Stanley Cup final on the road.

The Toronto Maple Leafs defeated the Detroit Red Wings 2-1 in game seven at the Olympia in Detroit on April 22, 1945 to capture the Stanley Cup. The Black Hawks were defeated in the Chicago Stadium on May 18, 1971, when the Montreal Canadiens won the Stanley Cup in the seventh game of that series. The home team has won the deciding game in ten of the twelve times that a best-of-seven final has gone the distance.

11. Name the only visiting team to win a game in New Jersey in the 2003 Stanley Cup playoffs.

The Ottawa Senators defeated the New Jersey Devils 2-1 in overtime in game six of the Eastern Conference final on May 21, 2003. Chris Phillips scored the overtime winner. This was the only home loss for the New

Jersey Devils during the 2003 playoffs. The Devils sported a record of twelve wins and one loss at home en route to their Stanley Cup celebration. The Devils set a record for the most home wins in a playoff year with these twelve victories.

12. When is the only time that the same two NHL teams met in three straight Stanley Cup final series?

The Montreal Canadiens and Detroit Red Wings faced off for three years in a row in 1954 through 1956. The Wings won in 1954 and 1955 and the Canadiens captured the Cup in 1956.

13. Name the only NHL team to win the Stanley Cup on the road in three consecutive years.

The Montreal Canadiens won the Cup on the road in three consecutive years. The Habs won the Stanley Cup at Philadelphia on May 16, 1976 with a 5-3 win over the Flyers. They then had Stanley Cup-winning games in Boston for two consecutive seasons. They defeated the Boston Bruins 2-1 in overtime on May 14, 1977 and then eliminated the Bruins in a 4-1 game played on May 25, 1978.

14. Name the first American-based NHL franchise to win the Stanley Cup.

The 1927-28 New York Rangers were playing in their second NHL season when they defeated the Montreal Maroons in a best-of-five series that went the limit. Prior to the NHL, the first American-based team to have won the Stanley Cup was the 1916-17 Seattle Metropolitans of the Pacific Coast Hockey Association.

15. What two teams played in the only Stanley Cup final between two Canadian-based NHL franchises that did not involve the Montreal Canadiens?

The Montreal Maroons defeated the Toronto Maple Leafs in a three game sweep to claim the Stanley Cup in the 1935 final.

16. How many times have six different NHL teams won the Stanley Cup in six consecutive years?

This has happened on only two occasions. Each of six years between 1931 to 1936 and 1992 to 1997 saw different Stanley Cup winners.

1931 Montreal Canadiens	1992 Pittsburgh Penguins
1932 Toronto Maple Leafs	1993 Montreal Canadiens
1933 New York Rangers	1994 New York Rangers
1934 Chicago Black Hawks	1995 New Jersey Devils
1935 Montreal Maroons	1996 Colorado Avalanche
1936 Detroit Red Wings	1997 Detroit Red Wings

17. Name the only team to skate in a preliminary playoff series in the 1970s and go on to play in a Stanley Cup final that year.

The 1978-79 New York Rangers eliminated the Los Angeles Kings in the final year of best-of-three preliminary playoff action. The Rangers then eliminated Philadelphia in the quarter-final and the Islanders in the semi-final. They were then defeated by the Montreal Canadiens.

18. Name the four NHL franchises that have both won and lost a game seven in a Stanley Cup final.

Team	Winning Year(s)	Losing Year(s)
Detroit Red Wings	1950, 1954, 1955	1942, 1945, 1964
Montreal Canadiens	1965, 1971	1954, 1955
New York Rangers	1994	1950
New Jersey Devils	2003	2001

19. How many NHL players have scored Stanley Cup-winning goals in consecutive years?

Only two individuals have scored the Cup winner in consecutive years. Jack Darragh of the Ottawa Senators was the first NHL player to do so. He scored Cup-winning goals against both the Seattle Metropolitans in 1920 and the Vancouver Millionaires the following year. The most recent player to accomplish this was Mike Bossy of the New York Islanders. He scored the Stanley Cup winner in 1982 while facing the Vancouver Canucks and followed it with another winner in 1983 against the Edmonton Oilers.

20. Name the most recent player to score a Stanley Cup-winning goal in his final NHL game.

Jacques Lemaire scored the winning goal in the Canadiens' 4-1 victory over the New York Rangers on May 21, 1979, when the Canadiens took the Cup in five games. Lemaire went on to play and coach in Switzerland for two seasons. He then returned to North America as a coach.

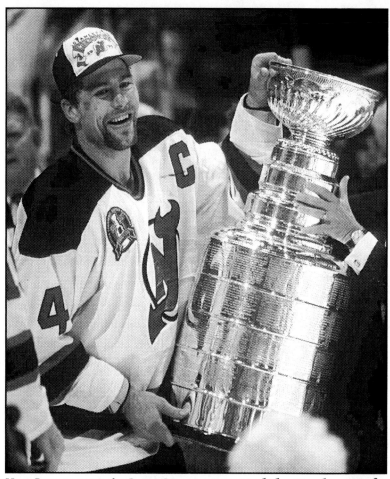

New Jersey captain Scott Stevens accepted the Stanley Cup for the first time in 1995.

PHOTO REPLAY

1. Name the six players who were members of the New Jersey Stanley Cup-winning team in both 1995 and 2003.

Tommy Albelin, Martin Brodeur, Sergei Brylin, Ken Daneyko, Scott Niedermayer and Scott Stevens all skated with the Devils in both of these seasons. Of these six, only Tommy Albelin was not a member of the other New Jersey Cup winner in 2000.

2. Name the only captain, at the end of the 2002-03 NHL season, who had been serving in that role longer than Scott Stevens.

Steve Yzerman became the captain of the Detroit Red Wings for the 1986-87 season. Scott Stevens took on the role of captain with the New Jersey Devils in 1992-93. Joe Sakic has also served as captain since 1992-93 with the Quebec Nordiques/Colorado Avalanche.

3. How many defensemen have won the Conn Smythe Trophy?

There have been seven defensemen who have won the Conn Smythe Trophy since it was first awarded in 1965.

Conn Smythe Trophy-Winning Defensemen

Year	Player	Team
1969	Serge Savard	Montreal Canadiens
1970, 1972	Bobby Orr	Boston Bruins
1978	Larry Robinson	Montreal Canadiens
1989	Al MacInnis	Calgary Flames
1994	Brian Leetch	New York Rangers
2000	Scott Stevens	New Jersey Devils
2002	Nicklas Lidstrom	Detroit Red Wings

4. Name the four individuals who have played in the most Stanley Cup playoff games to the end of the 2003 playoffs.

Patrick Roy, Mark Messier, Claude Lemieux and Scott Stevens are the all-time leaders in NHL playoff games played, following the 2003 Stanley Cup playoffs. Patrick Roy had participated in 247 playoff games when he announced his retirement in May of 2003. Mark Messier is second, having played in 236 playoff games. Scott Stevens and Claude Lemieux are tied for third with 233 appearances.